I Choose To Continue

Bobbie Glaze Custer

QUOTES FROM READERS

"An extraordinary story of courage, love and indomitable energy...a remarkable tale with a very personal and heartwarming narrative."

Jerome Stone, Founding President
National Alzheimer's Assoc., Chicago, Illinois

"Will await copies of your book for distribution at the Alzheimer's International Conference...a moving book."

Brian Moss, President
Alzheimer's Society of Australia

"I didn't move until I finished your book...so much I could relate to...after my divorce I felt complete failure...you made my heart sing."

Anonymous

"Congratulations to you...one of the best volunteer achievers ever!"

John Mack Carter, Editor, Good House Keeping

"A beautiful book...Like sitting across the table talking to you!"

Marie Andrews, Burnsville, Minnesota

"Thank you for sharing...a moving book,...a gift for presenting both tragic and gently humorous experiences...memorable description."

Dr. Norman Bansen, Dana College, Blair, Nebraska

"Glad you were persuaded to write your story...you are a great trailblazer."

Grace du Faur, Tauranga, New Zealand

"This story of Bobbie's life 'so far' has all the ingredients of a made-for-TV-movie. An 'ordinary' housewife from a small town in South Dakota took on the marathon task of caring for a husband with Alzheimer's disease and helping other such families when few in the medical profession knew what the disease was. This is a warm and tender story of my most remarkable friend."

Frances Cooper Thompson
Historian for the International P.E.O. Sisterhood
Former Archivist for Norman Cousins

PREFACE

We need to know how others have experienced happiness and we need to know how they have coped with sadness or tragedy. We grow by sharing with others. The last verse of a favorite poem, "Sharing", by an anonymous writer, says it all:

"There isn't much that I can do
but I can share my friends with you,
and I can share my life with you,
and oft'times share a prayer too--
as on our way we go."

These pages are a capsule-attempt to mirror my life so that you, my family, or interested others, may better know and understand me. It is my hope that this book may bring a measure of reassurance, joy or encouragement to the reader.

Manufactured in the United States of America

Printed by Lakeland Color Press

Cover design by Bruce Moulton

BGC Publishing Company
9550 Collegeview Road
Bloomington, MN 55437

Publishing Coordinator: Jody Smeby

ACKNOWLEDGEMENTS

I am grateful to all who have touched my life, many of whom are named in this "open book". To Ken, with whom I shared many years, and together, nurtured our family. I sincerely feel that unknowingly, he made a great contribution toward helping others and creating awareness regarding Alzheimer's Disease and related disorders. His tragic and untimely illness brought about my desire to become involved with those struggling against all odds and to share a loving, caring concern. To our daughters, Sharee and Mitzi, who have shown strength and have been a constant support. To their children - my grandchildren - Jody, Mark, Benjamin and Ian, who have been the light of my life. To Gordon, a remarkable, sensitive, beautiful man who actually saved my life and made it all worthwhile, even in the darkest moments. And to our expanded family - his children - Kay and Michael, who have accepted me and shown their approval which has meant so much to me. Their children - Gordon's grandchildren - David, Steven, Aaron and Bret, have been easy to think of as my additional grandchildren. All of those named have enriched my life. It is with love and appreciation that I dedicate this book to them.

A special "thank you" to my dear and loyal friend, Fran, without whose encouragement this writing would not have become a reality.

1

It was a difficult beginning - coming into the "cold world" in the middle of a blizzard in a small town, Pipestone, Minnesota. I can remember my mother telling how she walked to the hospital several blocks away in 30 degree below zero weather. There was far too much snow on the ground to back a car out of the garage, so she and my father slowly trudged through snow drifts that sparkled like diamonds and crackled crisply under every footstep. They made periodic stops as mother took a deep breath and felt another pain, which told her that soon she would be delivering a brand new little someone. Dad had secretly hoped for a little girl (I've been told that fathers usually think of daughters as very special) and besides, he already had a boy. Another baby boy, Marcus, had died in infancy.

And so it was, that I made my grand entrance, tipping the scales at just short of five pounds with all my clothes on. Dad's pet name for my mother was "Sis", (don't ask me why) and he would hold my little hand in his and say adoringly, "Sis, her little finger isn't much larger than the lead in a pencil."

I'm sure I must have sensed that I was surrounded by love even at that early date, for in addition to fond parents, I was blessed with a proud, protective brother, Frederic, who was five years old.

I was six weeks old when our family chose to move back to Wolsey, South Dakota, where Mother and Dad had been raised and lived during their early years of marriage.

The close relationship with my brother continued through the years, even though, as most brothers do, he simply loved to tease. I'm sure I was a bothersome sister and a nuisance at times. His favorite trick was to take me down on the floor, sit on my feet, hold my hands, and chew my ears! Oh, how I hated that feeling, all yukky and wet! However, he was delighted as I kicked and squealed. I'm sure my shrieks could be heard all over the neighborhood. Even at that, I always wanted to play "cops and robbers" with him and his friends or be in on whatever they were doing. It was during one of these times that I begged to play leap-frog with them, and although the protests were many, they reluctantly allowed me to join them. On my first attempt, over I went and landed just right with my left wrist doubled under me. I heard and felt the loud crack, and my howls filled the air. Needless to say, the game stopped abruptly, as a frightened, but at the same time, disgusted big brother took me home to my mother. Perhaps it was just a sprain, she thought, so it was carefully bound to make it more comfortable. Not so. There was very little sleep that night as the pain become more severe, and finally it was necessary to remove the binding due to increased swelling.

The next morning, as soon as possible, Mother took me to the home of our small-town doctor, where he proceeded to seat me on a piano bench in their "parlor" and set my broken wrist by giving it a quick unexpected twist. I had never fainted, but the room whirled and spun as I caught my breath trying to recover from the excruciating pain. I learned very early that suffering is a part of life.

I was fortunate to have family nearby who played a large part in my life, especially my "growing up years". My father's brother, Uncle Ott, and wife, Aunt Emma, cousins Conrad and Robert Newton, lived directly across the street from us. The two brothers were in business together, owning and operating Newton Brothers Store, but our family "get-togethers" were only at Thanksgiving, Christmas and New Year's. We alternated having these family dinners at one or the other's home. It was a very special time with turkey and all the trimmings shared by our two families. The singing and games later in the day were great fun and enjoyed by all.

Others in my father's family were sisters Min and Lou. Unfortunately, there was not an opportunity to know them and their families. Three step-brothers from another marriage were just people that we were told existed, but we knew little about them.

Mother's sister, Aunt Berte, was a strong influence in my life, especially with her love of music and poetry. She and Mother sang duets beautifully just as they had done all their lives. Both played the piano also and they would make "beautiful music together", much of which they themselves composed. (Mother began playing for church when she was eleven years old.) Aunt Berte's visits were rather infrequent because of the distance and the transportation, but they were such a joy. Her Christmas package was always full of surprises, but we could be sure there would be a pomegranate for each of us. They were a unique treat, for it was the only time we had them.

Aunt Berte's boys, Stan and Joe, were always thrilled to come from the city to visit their "country cousins". It was a rare trip for them to sit a friend's farm and see all the farm animals and machinery. How we laughed when they were watching for the first time as the farmer milked a cow. Joe looked puzzled and asked innocently, "Which handle does the cream come from?"

In turn, there were a few memorable trips to Minneapolis for us to visit Aunt Berte and the boys. What a thrill it was for a little country girl to ride the streetcars, visit Excelsior Amusement Park and attend some beautiful theaters. The theaters then had "live entertainment" with dancing girls, a "real" orchestra, and many times a pipe organ that would fill the auditorium with its music. It seemed I must be dreaming. I cherished every moment in such a beautiful place with its statues, marble stairs and crystal chandeliers.

My grandfather Newton (Henry) was born in Michigan in 1842 and came to Wolsey in 1881. He filed a claim northeast of town and his first home was under a wagon. He later brought lumber from Michigan and built a beautiful home on his property. He dug the first artesian well in town. His family joined him in 1884. His wife, Lillian (my grandmother), whom he married when she was 15 years of age, died at age 29. He remarried, but the new stepmother was unkind to my father and the other children. They all left home at an early age.

Of course, I never saw or knew my father's parents as they were already gone, but some of my richest and most precious memories are of my mother's parents, Grandma and Grandpa Campbell. Because I was the only granddaughter, I believe Grandpa thought surely I was a princess. At any rate, he made me feel like one. I was always perfectly content to stay with them at any time.

Grandpa wasn't afraid of anything. He loved to pheasant hunt, and one day while hunting with friends in a wagon drawn by horses, they went over a railroad track. The jolt caused his gun to discharge and the bullet went through his shoulder so close to his heart that one could see it beating. The friends brought him home and with help he walked upstairs to where they lived above his drug store. In later years, he hunted rattlesnakes on the bluffs along the Missouri River at Pierre, South Dakota, refusing to even wear boots for protection. He was quite a man.

Grandma had a beautiful voice and could usually be heard humming as she went about her housework. Her Irish wit showed through at unexpected times. Our family constantly remind each other of some of her favorite quotes, and laugh with much affection as we think of that dear little grandmother. She would sometimes say, "I must go now or Dave will have a worm with a green eye." When she was pleased with a project she had completed, she'd say, "Well, we're all done, buttoned up and back in the buggy."

Grandma always kept her sense of humor. When she was placed in a nursing home, she shared a room with another lady. One day as the commode (portable toilet) was wheeled in for her roommate to use, Grandma said to her, "Arise, Jupiter, and snuff the moon." The nurses were in stitches! When apologizing for a bit of dust on the furniture, she would say, "Well, if it's your own dirt, it's friendly." She once told me that she'd always believed in the advice to keep your mouth shut and your bowels open!

Grandma's nickname for me was "Bob-o-link" and Grandpa in a singing fashion, would say to me, "Bobbie Newton went a scootin'." (I guess I never did sit still for long.) Grandma always told me to "look out for Number One" and that the devil would never get me. I guess she figured I'd find some way out of difficulty. Obviously, we shared something very special.

Birthdays were not a big deal in our family except that there was always a birthday cake made by my mother--an angel food "made from scratch" that required using 13 egg whites. That's a lot of egg whites that had to be beaten stiff so that the cake would rise very high. Mother and I usually took turns operating the rotary beater as our arms became very tired. As a rule, a little friend whose birthday was the same day would come for a "birthday supper" or I might be invited to her home. I never did have a birthday party, for my father said we couldn't invite everyone, and because he was in business, he did not want anyone to feel left out.

Christmas was a treasured time--the beauty of the season, excitement in the air, rehearsals for Christmas programs at school and church, special days of preparation for festive holiday dinners. It is strange the things that stand out in our minds as children. The best china and cut glass were carefully taken out of the "china closet" (a curved glass cupboard which elegantly displayed these very special treasures) and the white linen tablecloths and napkins in cut glass napkin rings were carefully placed on the large oval oak table.

Mother prepared many dishes that were served exclusively at holiday time, for example, escalloped oysters and homemade cranberry sauce. Cranberries were cooked and put through a colander, sugar was added and then cooked again until it thickened. No one ever thought of such a thing as canned cranberry sauce. It was always served in crystal stemmed sherbet dishes topped with a dab of real whipped cream. It looked so pretty on the table and it was just the right touch with the turkey. Also there were individual cut glass "salts" at each place for it was always important to dip celery in salt. Mother made her own mince meat for the pies and the added few drops of brandy in it made it especially tasty.

Joy was a key word at this season. The gift of love was heard through the awesome Christmas story and the tableaux of the Holy family, I shall never forget. It made me realize the significance of Christmas.

When Santa Claus appeared at the close of our programs and had "treats" (sacks of candy and an apple) for all the children, there was suspense, even though at one time, I was afraid when he appeared and I hid under the chairs. I soon learned there was nothing ominous about Santa Claus!

Our Christmas tree was a family project with everyone joining in the decorating. We left our tree up as long as it had any needles on it. Christmas Eve, we all went to bed early and at daybreak, Mother would call us to let us know that it was time to don our slippers and robes and go downstairs. The fact that we were leaving a lovely warm "feather bed" under us and lots of warm hand-tied quilts for covers didn't deter us one bit. We sprang up and scurried down the open stairway where it was absolutely magic! The tree, all lighted in splendor, was too much mystery for a little girl to fathom. Special secrets had been hidden for such a long time. The charm of it all never left me.

Mother and Dad were wonderful examples for their children for they instilled in us how important it was to love and care. We learned about sharing and reverence for life. I am grateful to have had such a family.

2

Wonderful people lived in our small town.

I must tell you about "Doc" Cogswell and his family. He was a typical country doctor who was meticulous, steady, kind and gentle. With limited access to medical supplies, he simply did the best he could. He was extremely knowledgeable and dedicated. As to his profession, a good share of it was learned the hard way - from experience in a small community. It was not unusual for him in winter to travel many miles in a bobsled drawn by a team of horses, through a blinding blizzard at below zero temperatures to save a life or deliver a baby. Usually the baby arrived in the family farmhouse where the only heat might be a wood-burning stove and the only light a kerosene lamp. "Doc" was admired by everyone, and the entire community and surrounding territory depended on his "being there" when necessary.

Doc had an unusual assistant in the person of his compassionate, loving wife. Now Mable was some lady. There wasn't a soul who did not love and respect her. She was a "pied piper" to all the young people and took time to listen if there was a problem or someone needed help. She was a real "pro" when it came to emergencies. Many times farmers would be brought to the doctor's home to find that "Doc" was out on a "call". Perhaps an arm or leg might have been caught in farm machinery and mangled. No matter what the circumstances were, Mable "kept her cool". She would clean and bandage the wound, try to make the patient as comfortable as possible, and reassure him until "Doc" could be reached. She really was a Florence Nightingale.

Yes, Mable was an inspiration and a delight to know, for her fun-loving creativity seemed to work overtime. I'm sure there never was a school or church program that she did not have a hand in, whether it was costumes, scenery, music or direction. She could make what seemed to us a "regal gown" for Cinderella, when the only materials there were to work with were two "very used" old lace curtains, a bit of braid or ribbon and a touch of Christmas tinsel for the glistening touch that a royal princess would need. I was in the fourth grade and I can remember (for I played the part of Cinderella) the "oh's" and "ah's" from the audience as I made my first appearance in such an elegant and "elaborate" costume. Mable and Doc's son Mark, who took a good deal of convincing, played the prince and looked stunning in his purple plumed hat, purple-dyed bloomers and his sister Maxine's silk stockings! He was so chagrined that when it was time for the "picture-taking" of this "outstanding" production, Mark deliberately looked cross-eyed in every picture, which more than dismayed his mother.

The doctor's home was always open to all and even the weekly choir practice took place there with Mable directing and daughter, Maxine, accompanying. Choir was never thought of as a "duty" for it was always a special time. Goodies and treats were usually provided. After the serious anthem-singing, the rugs were rolled back, and Maxine transformed the piano into an instrument that nearly jumped up and down. All of us teenagers loved to dance, and because we were not allowed to have school dances, this weekly ritual was something to which we all looked forward. It was fun! We were all faithful and dependable, never failing to take our place in the choir on Sunday morning at the Presbyterian Church, which was simply a basement built by the men in the community (including my father). Our minister was a woman, believe it or not, long before we'd heard of "women's lib". Her name was Famy B. Mills and she was somewhat of a character, but always sincere. We kids had a difficult time keeping straight faces when she sang, almost bellowing. She had her favorite hymns of course, such as "Jesus, like a shepherd lead us." She literally "swooped" up and down on the word "lead" and we didn't dare look at each other. I remember wondering why the funniest things always seemed to happen during the most serious moments in church. Years later, when money became available, the structure was completed. I never had the opportunity to attend church services in a real church in Wolsey.

The Cogswell family had a tremendous influence on the community and our family in particular. We shared fishing trips, traveling at least 25 miles over dirt or graveled roads to spend a day at a lake. Autos could not travel very fast so it seemed quite a distance. The lakes were actually small ponds where Dad and Doc might catch a few crappies or bluegills, but more than likely, if anything, they had to be satisfied with a few bullheads.

Our mothers were in charge of our picnic lunch which somehow was to us the most important part of our day. We kids swam in the mucky water and explored the territory where we were careful not to walk into poison ivy. Sometimes we all came home with a bad case of chiggers - oh, how they itched! We were sunburned, dirty, tired, and a sight to behold, but it was a memorable time.

We went on hunting and camping trips, too, that were never to be forgotten. We even traveled to the Black Hills of South Dakota and that was something! It was an adventure to go that far (300 miles) from home. Our two families stayed in a log cabin on the side of a wooded hill with a mountain stream below. With my eyes closed, I can still smell the pine trees and the burning campfire as we gathered round each evening. Nights became very cool, so we snuggled into flannel pajamas and warm socks with a whole pile of comforters on our beds. During the day, chipmunks scurried across the porch, hurdling over our collection of beautiful Black Hills stones and rocks which we had gathered the previous day. The bits of mica in each stone reflected a myriad of colors. The air was crisp and exhilarating, and sometimes we could see our breath in the early morning.

Our menu every meal, every day, consisted of baked beans on pancakes. And this was for one whole week! Believe it or not, we were lined up and ready at mealtime and it tasted great!

One day, our car ran over and killed a huge rattlesnake. Some might say that it was beautiful with its many colors of the rainbow, but somehow I didn't share that feeling. "Doc" gave us a lesson though, revealing to us the 12 rattles on its tail and explaining to us the workings of the fangs by propping the mouth open with a stick. It is a vivid memory. Later,the snake skin was made into a belt for Maxine. Glad it wasn't for me!

Another camping experience, quite different, occurred when our two families drove a distance of nearly 30 miles so that the two Dads could go grouse hunting. We pitched our large tent in a pasture with not one tree in sight. This area was known as Wessington Hills. After a scrumptious supper of fried potatoes, corn on the cob cooked in the husks, and hamburgers done over an open fire, it was time to think about "hitting the hay" literally and figuratively, for we had stopped at a farmhouse nearby and asked if we might have a bit of hay to lay on the ground under our blankets. Naturally, we weren't accustomed to sleeping on such a hard surface. Our "beds" were rather unique, for the two mothers slept in the middle, each having her family beside her. Eight of us in a row! How fun! As soon as it became dark, it was "Doc's" signal to begin telling his detailed, descriptive hair-raising ghost stories - another one of his famous talents. I can remember moving closer to mother to hold her hand as I trembled with fright. There was welcome relief when the story ended and all was well.

At daybreak, we were awakened by the sounds of whoops, hollers and tom-toms. You can well imagine how we felt out on that lonely countryside. Dad quickly pulled on his trousers and made his way to the farmhouse to inquire if we were about to be attacked, only to find that it was a friendly band of Indians in full-feathered attire rehearsing for an exhibition they were to present at the South Dakota State Fair about 30 miles away. Thank heavens! Yes, Doc's family meant a lot to us.

Another special family was the depot agent, Jim, his wife, Ottie, and their adopted daughter, Edna (her nickname was "Tootie"). We were next-door neighbors. Ottie was a large woman with a generous heart. She was a marvelous Scandinavian cook and kept us well supplied with unusual Norwegian surprises such as delicious krumkake and fatiman. Jim loved to play the fiddle and didn't have to be asked to play if someone would accompany him on the piano (usually my mother). The first radio I ever saw or heard was in a room upstairs over the depot where Jim was depot agent. They invited us there to hear a musical program broadcast from Minneapolis. It seemed incredible that from that small box in Wolsey, South Dakota, we could listen to a program 300 miles away in Minneapolis! The static was so bad that we strained to hear even part of it, but it was unforgettable. The world seemed to become smaller as news could travel much faster than it had in the past.

Tootie was a very nervous little girl and was the unfortunate victim of an accident when she was very young. She was walking down the street with her mother when she suddenly let loose of her mother's hand and ran into the street. At that moment, a runaway team of horses pulling a wagon struck her down and the wagon ran over and crushed her foot. She was to be a cripple the rest of her life. Mother would say to me, "Be nice to Tootie because she is handicapped and needs help." When she first started school, I went for her each day and pulled her in a little red wagon. It was a beautiful lesson initiated by my mother, in finding the joy of helping others.

Tootie and I played together every day and one of our favorite times was when our old mother cat, Blackie, had kittens. This event seemed to take place as often as possible and what excitement! Blackie, who was actually <u>all</u> colors, would find her way back in a very small crawl space that was meant to be a drain for water to run off the porch of our house.

There she would have her litter of kittens. How she ever managed that in such a small space, I could never figure out, but it was certain that it was her "delivery room". I remember how we reached back as far as we could to carefully bring out each furry little wiggly creature - so tiny and soft and helpless. And what fun it was to discover the color of the next one - generally, each was different. We immediately chose names for them and there was always a favorite. We played with them by the hour, dressing them in doll clothes, and wheeling them around in our doll buggies.

There was one family who lived near us that were exceptional friends also - "Abie" and Mable Custer and son Gordon. Abie's initials were A. B., hence the nickname. He was a mail carrier and drove by our house every day, ready to begin his "rural route". He was a kind, gentle man and was never to be daunted by the severe South Dakota weather. The farmers knew he would see that they received their mail. Abie and Dad played ball together (in their spare time) on the "town team". They shared mutual admiration for each other. Mable, no bigger than a minute, stopped in at our house each time she walked to the store. She was extremely sensitive to the beautiful things in life, even to keeping her house in spotless condition. Her handwork was done to perfection. She made me a pair of "cut-work" pillow cases for my hope-chest, which years later seemed a strange coincidence. This mother and dad were unusual parents, teaching their son Gordon the value of education and how to make the most of his talents and capabilities. He, too, was often at our house with other pals of my brother and me. We were great friends.

Small town folks in the midwest were the greatest, for they were like one big family, all concerned for the others, sharing, helping out in time of need, and even though we knew the necessity of sacrifice, we were content and happy.

3

Wolsey's Main Street was typical of most towns of its size. Supermarkets didn't exist. An important part of "downtown", especially in smaller towns, were "general stores". My father and his brothers were proprietors of Newton Bros. Store, which was originally established and the business started by their father - a real pioneer, my Grandfather Newton.

In the general store there were many items besides groceries. There were "dry goods" (sewing materials and notions), hardware, clothing, shoes, etc. Sometimes when working there, I would measure off several yards of cloth for a customer and go from there to the back of the store to fill a kerosene can or a vinegar jug. Most groceries came by bulk, so it was necessary to weigh perhaps five pounds of sugar or potatoes, a pound of lard, or 10¢ worth of rice. Nothing was pre-packaged except canned goods. Everything else was "sacked".

Newton Bros. Store was a place where farmers brought their eggs in crates and sold them to the merchants in exchange for groceries. The eggs had to be "candled" to make sure they were not spoiled. This was done by holding each egg to a small hole in a box which contained a light bulb. If the egg appeared to be clear it was ok, but if it looked dark or cloudy it was thrown out. A slip was placed in the empty egg crate, telling the number of "good eggs" so that the farmer would know how much money he could plan on for groceries. A small sack of candy was always placed in the egg crate as a special bonus for the children. The job of "candling" was usually assigned to me and I disliked it with a passion. It was done in a small, poorly lighted room, without a window for ventilation. It was extremely hot in summer, and I'd much rather have been with my friends. Once in a while, I was excused so that I could join them.

Also on Main Street there was a pool hall, post office, barber shop, lumber-yard, bank, cafe, bakery, drugstore, elevator, meat market, and a filling station. Grandpa Campbell was the druggist in earlier years as my mother was growing up.

Farmers came to town Saturday nights and parked their cars diagonally in the center of Main Street. They went about finding other farmers and friends for it was a social time for visiting.

Sometimes there would be a band concert in the bandstand on Main Street. There were also public dances held in the old "Opera House". It had that name because it had been used for traveling shows and plays and other "cultural events" that came to town on occasion. It was an experience to attend the dances because there were always "drunks" and more than likely a fight or two, but with so little for young folks to do, we always looked forward to them. My mother usually chaperoned a group of girls, and she would sit back in a corner so as not to spoil our fun or embarrass me. Rarely did anyone "date", for very few boys had money enough for two people. The music was many times provided by local, self-taught "musicians" but occasionally, a "real orchestra" was brought to town. It was a special treat when Lawrence Welk came there with his five-piece orchestra that was newly organized and broadcast regularly over station WNAX at Yankton, South Dakota.

Another feature that took place at the Opera House was "once in a while movies". These were silent movies that flashed speaking parts on the screen after each picture. My father started this "movie house" and to make it more "real life" he acquired several "sound" records - one was a train, one an airplane, love songs, etc. He placed me in charge of making sure that the correct sound record was in place on the "talking machine" or "phonograph" at the time there was a train on the screen, or whichever was the appropriate sound. It wasn't unusual for me to have the sound of cannons booming in the middle of a love scene. This was another of my most un-favorite jobs, even though I knew I was expected to share in the work of the family - a good learning experience.

There were two railroads, the Milwaukee and the North-western, running through town. In early days salesmen traveled by train and many times had to change trains in order to get to their destination. A wood-frame hotel, built by my Grandfather Newton in early years, had its place on Main Street until a fire burned an entire block and left the hotel nothing but a pile of ashes. It was a major catastrophe to the community. However, businesses were rebuilt and continued as usual very soon. No one ever thought of "giving up".

Our town had a small (but outstanding to us) swimming pool built by the townspeople. Naturally, it was the most popular place in summer. The water and drainage system were most inadequate (a one-inch pipe brought water into the pool from an artesian well). There was one small overflow. It didn't matter to us how thick and green the water became.

Why we didn't all die of some horrible disease, I'll never know, for it was only possible to drain and clean the pool once during the summer months (it took a week to fill it). But out on that prairie in 100 degree heat with hardly any shade trees, it was an absolute oasis! Nearby at a filling station was a very small building that we called the "pop house", where soda pop and ice cream were sold for a nickel (if anyone was lucky enough to have a nickel - we knew nothing of "allowances".) One could always find young people at this so-called "hangout" where we made plans such as a hike out on the cemetery road or perhaps a watermelon feed on the schoolhouse hill in the moonlight. It was a happy time.

Once in a while a carnival came to town where a ferris wheel and a merry-go-round were set up on Main Street. We sometimes had a parade with the Wolsey Town Band and a few (very few) "floats" - (perhaps a few cars or trucks decorated with crepe paper). There weren't many cars in our town.

Every summer we could expect a visit from a band of gypsies passing through town. There were four or five automobiles, much finer than any in town, with generally one man who was the "boss", a number of women, and a lot of children. They dressed in colorful clothing, the girls in long dresses and lots of jewelry. The man wore overalls with a bright neckerchief. He always had a full beard. They stopped downtown and scattered in all directions, begging. Storekeepers and businesses had to watch carefully for they would "steal you blind", people said. They moved on to the next town after an hour or so.

If a fire should break out in town, someone ran to ring the firebell. Our volunteer fire department, which consisted of nearly every man in town, came running from all directions to help. A small cart on two large wagon wheels carrying a fire hose was pulled by the men to the location of the fire and it was connected to a fire plug. Our water supply was stored in a tall water tower that could be seen from quite a distance. Sometimes the fire could be contained and extinguished before too much damage, but other times it was impossible to save a building. Prairie fires were also a threat, and many times it would be several days before it could be brought under control.

Our "police department" was one man called a marshall, whose duty it was to keep law and order. He was also in charge of the water supply and the sewer system. We did not worry much about break-ins or violence in our sleepy little hometown, so his was a rather easy life. We felt safe enough that we rarely locked our doors or the cars on the street. It was a very secure environment in which to grow up.

There was no such thing as a dairy, but milk was delivered twice a week by our "milk man" who milked his own cow. The milk was not pasteurized, but it was poured into sterilized bottles and brought to our door. The "cream" went to the top of the bottle and that was usually poured off carefully so we could use that on our "breakfast food" rather than the "blue" milk underneath. This was a sideline for our milkman, for he was also the town banker. He was valuable to our town.

The old "light plant" provided all of the electricity for the community. It consisted of a coal-fired boiler which produced steam to run the generator. Farmers had no electricity and depended on kerosene lamps for light.

Each family was responsible for disposing of their garbage and refuse. Some was burned in homemade burners in our yards, but the rest was hauled to the "town dump" where it was also burned. Sometimes it was necessary to bury it but if not, it smoldered for days and left a putrid odor.

There were no funeral homes in Wolsey, so when someone died, the body was embalmed and placed in a casket which was left open in the "parlor" of the home until the funeral (usually three days). A "wake" was held when neighbors took turns sitting with the body all night, and friends could come by for a "reviewal" and discuss whether the corpse looked good or bad. Funerals were lengthy and ghastly with generally a long sermon and the obituary giving an account of the deceased's fine deeds. It was usually "flowery" whether or not it was true. Favorite hymns, such as "Abide With Me" and "The Old Rugged Cross" were sung by a local mixed quartette (usually off-key). Burial took place at the cemetery two miles east of town. There were no trees - just tombstones, bare and desolate. It was a lonely place. We kids thought it was "spooky".

School was where the action took place - both for learning and socially. We were very proud of our school. There were some excellent teachers and some others that we could have done without. One favorite, Miss Peck, inspired me and aroused my interest in writing and poetry that never left me. There were high standards and some outstanding students were the result. Not many of us had an opportunity to pursue education beyond high school. Most had to find jobs.

Athletics (chiefly basketball) were a top priority. It was very important to win but there was emphasis on character-building and good sportsmanship as well. There was a real rivalry between our town and other towns of its size. Sometimes there weren't enough players in high school for the team, so then recruits were taken along from the upper grades. Physical training was required and if a player was caught smoking, he was immediately taken off the team. As a cheerleader, I never missed a game. Our chant, "Strawberry shortcake, blueberry pie, V-I-C-T-O-R-Y. Are we in it? Well, I guess. Wolsey High School - yes - yes - Yes!" echoed over the din of the loyal fans. A basketball game was an event! And all of this in a small gymnasium where there was hardly room to turn around. At times our team played a game in the upper floor of a store building when we played away from home. It would be difficult for our grandchildren to believe this.

We had lots of music in our schools with our glee clubs and especially our orchestra of 26 members. I played first violin and have regretted that I didn't keep on with it. Our big thrill came when we took first place in the State Music Contest! We were even invited to Huron, 15 miles away, to perform for their Chamber of Commerce. It was quite an undertaking for all of us with our instruments to be transported there for that occasion. It was worth it. The "Evening Huronite" even gave an account of our performance and the honor we had received. We were in the big time!

There weren't many outstanding "happenings", but one was the State Fair which was held annually in nearby Huron on the State Fairground. There wasn't much activity in Wolsey during Fair Week. I cannot adequately describe the excitement of this event with all of its special buildings and booths with displays of horticulture, agriculture, women's and men's arts and crafts, homemaking and school exhibits. So much to see! Even the livestock buildings and the farm animals of all kinds with their young, held special intrigue. These animals were judged as were the other exhibits such as hand-work, baked goods, jellies and jams. Prizes to be treasured were given. The various sounds of the midway with hawkers peddling their wares of brightly colored and spangled souvenirs, and the smell of popcorn and hot dogs seem like yesterday. The side shows, with everything from gaudy belly dancers to the "freak shows", where one could see the "wonders of the world" were a must. In the evening, the special event was the grandstand performance with music, dancing girls and a brilliant fireworks display. Terrific! Many times the evening ended at our house for coffee which simply extended an already unforgettable evening. We felt we were lucky kids.

It is true we didn't have much nor did we expect much, but we learned to appreciate the true values in life. Every child would benefit from being raised in a town such as ours, although our Main Street was not the most exciting place in the world to passers-by.

4

We lived a block from the railroad tracks, on Main Street, and many freight trains carrying grain and other supplies passed through town daily. These trains were usually a mile long. Times were tough in those years, and many "hobos" (transient men who were looking for farm work) "rode the rails" as we called it. The box cars were usually jammed with these people who sometimes jumped off long enough to knock on the doors of nearby homes and asked for food before catching the next train. Mother usually gave them some small chore to tend to while she made sandwiches and fixed lunch for them. I can't ever remember her turning one away to go hungry. It was a nearly daily ritual. Dad used to tease her and say that the house must be marked in some way, for they seemed to know it was a good bet for them.

We had no refrigerator for a long time, but we did have, like most others, a wooden icebox that had a separate compartment on top for a 50-pound chunk of ice. The ice was cut and taken from the "Jim" river and stored in an icehouse in sawdust until it would be delivered to our homes.

It was brought to our house and put in the ice box where we could use an icepick to chip off pieces for a cold drink. There was a pan placed underneath the box to catch the water as the ice melted. It was important, as you can well imagine, to remember once in a while to empty the pan so it wouldn't run over. It wasn't uncommon to have to mop up a puddle on the floor! What a day it was when we became the proud owners of an electric refrigerator with real ice cubes! I wasn't anxious to get very far from home after that.

There were few telephones. We did not have one in our home, as my father felt that that was an unnecessary luxury as long as there was one at our store. Besides, we were almost within shouting distance of friends we might wish to call. These marvelous inventions were oblong boxes attached to the wall. By turning a crank after the receiver was off the hook, we could give the number we were calling when the operator said, "Number please". It was simply magic. The switchboard where the operator sat had several plugs on cords that she put into the proper slots on the board, and suddenly there was the voice that you wanted to reach on the other end of the line. Sometimes there were five or six people on a "party line" who could "listen in" to other people's conversations. It was a way of entertainment for some and surely a good way to catch up on all the small town gossip.

Rain or shine, Monday was always "wash day". Early in the morning, Mother would light the two-burner kerosene stove in the basement. On it sat a copper boiler which we filled with pails of water. It took a long time to heat, but when it began steaming, we lifted pails of hot water into the washing machine. The white clothes had already been boiled and placed in the machine. When we felt the clothes were clean we stopped the machine and piece by piece put them through a "wringer" turned by hand. The clothes were then hung outside on a clothesline to dry. In winter they would freeze stiff before we could hang them on the line - our hands nearly froze, too. After a time, we brought them inside and many times had to finish drying them on a clothes rack. Oh, but they did smell wonderfully fresh!

For winter recreation, we often met at our house before walking several miles through ice and snow to Cane Creek to ice skate. In those days, our skates were the "clamp-on" type and were worn over a shoe and tightened with a skate key. Our hands nearly had icicles on them by the time we reached the creek and it was difficult to tighten our skates. We gathered cow chips (cow manure) to build a fire to keep us warm and tried to skate on the little winding, frozen creek that was full of humps and hollows. Indoor ice skating with shoe-skates and music were something we'd never even dreamed about.

Another wintertime thrill was sliding on our sleds down the schoolhouse hill. There was a trail to follow and it was thrilling to "fly" down the hill, trying to avoid wrapping the sled and ourselves around the trees which lined the path. This sometimes happened.

After these frigid winter sports, we often came to our house (or one of the other's homes) for popcorn or fudge or perhaps a taffy pull. Sometimes we had oyster stew. This was followed by dancing to records on a Victrola or phonograph. Someone had to stay close by to turn the crank so that the music didn't run down. Song fests were a favorite pastime as we gathered around the piano. Our hearts were filled with happiness even if our fun was "homemade".

In the summers, between our house and Tootie's, a group of girls would sometimes "sleep out" under the stars. We laid our blankets on the grass and we talked the night away. We had snacks and goodies and giggled as girls do. One morning at sunup, we thought we'd be daring and go swimming before anyone was around (we really wanted to go "skinny-dipping"). We wore our swim suits into the water and then took them off and placed them on the edge of the pool. We were really living dangerously! What we did not know was that one of the girls' brother and a friend knew of our plans. They stealthily crept up and snatched our suits and ran with them! Oh! We were furious! They taunted us for an hour or more until people began circulating around town. Finally, they gave us our suits so that we could get out of the water. We never forgave them for such a sneaky trick.

Our house was halfway between school and downtown, so it was naturally a "gathering place" for my friends in my earlier years. Our family all took pride in our home and we loved sharing it with others. From the pup tent in our back yard, which also had a tire swing on the big old cottonwood tree, to our open front porch with a railing that was such fun to jump over, and the old "bench" porch swing so inviting, topped off with the luscious smell of homemade bread or cookies baking, made our house a home which gave us cherished memories.

5

It has been said that "into every life a little rain must fall." As I reflect back upon the simple life of my childhood, I realize that in many ways it was extremely difficult. It is my belief that many of the hardships I "weathered" actually prepared me for reverses in later life. It is my philosophy that there is some good in everything. Given time and patience, we grow from experiencing sorrow and hard knocks.

While my childhood held many happy times and there was so much good that I enjoyed, there were also times of trouble that had a tremendous impact on my life. In looking back, I now realize how impressionable and sensitive children are to traumas that occur in families. Learning to "cope", often times must be learned early.

It was a warm summer day in mid-afternoon that I was summoned to come into the house. I had been playing in the yard when a neighbor called to me and said my father was ill and wanted to see me. Even at the early age of nine, I sensed something unusual and frightening about her tone of voice. I rather reluctantly and quietly entered the room where on the black leather couch, lay my father. He was gray in color and did not appear to be moving. I stepped up beside him and asked, "Daddy, are you feeling better?" He did not answer me, which was puzzling. As tears rolled down his face, I became aware that he could not speak. I was told my father had had a stroke. I had no idea what that meant except I knew it must be something terrible. What I did not realize was that at that moment my life would never be as it had been. My brother and I were told that we must be brave for Mother's sake. I suddenly felt very mature and responsible. No one explained to me that my father would be partially paralyzed for the rest of his days, or that he would have a personality change that would be bewildering to us. From that day on, I seemed to have a mental block as to the special good times that I was told my father and I shared. I only remembered how it was after he became ill.

Dad wanted just Mother to take care of him and was unreasonable and impatient. After ten days in bed, he decided he wanted to go downtown to the barber shop for a haircut. He was so determined, even knowing it had been forbidden by the doctor, that Mother hid his clothes. He called me to his room and ordered me to find his clothes and help him dress. I begged him not to exert himself. In a rage, he demanded that I obey him. I can remember how hard I cried when he left the house. It wasn't surprising that he was gone only a short time when two men drove him home and carried him into the house. He had had a more severe stroke while he was in the barber chair. The fact that I was the one who helped him with his clothes so that he could go, left a tremendous guilt load on a very small girl. I suffered with that, keeping my feelings to myself, for a very long time. I felt totally responsible.

There were times that Dad would be so depressed that he would not eat for several days. Mother would beg him to come to the table to eat with the family but he refused. I would lie awake at night listening for the thump of his cane. Many times he would get out of bed and work his way downstairs and sit in the dark. There were days that I would hide the sharp knives in the kitchen before I went to school, fearful for both my mother and father. Sometimes I went across the street and asked my aunt to please "look in" on Mother during the day. To this day I am terrified of strokes that may leave an active, productive individual brain-damaged to such an extent as that which left my father someone I scarcely recognized.

These changes in my father continued for a period of six years during which time our family routine was necessarily altered. This was beyond my understanding. Frequently there were days that were sad and lonely. Our family had always enjoyed music with Mother at the piano. My brother played trombone or drums (sometimes Dad played drums), and I played the violin. Mother and I loved playing piano duets also. I had really just begun piano lessons, but it became impossible to continue. It seemed to make Dad nervous and we were told to be quiet. The times when we could bring our friends home were fewer and had to be arranged when my father had gone upstairs to bed or would be away from the house.

In 1929 the depression began and everyone felt the crunch as banks began to close and people lost everything they had in savings. We all knew the true meaning of hard times. Everyone was in the "same boat" so to speak, so we tightened our belts and carried on. It was a lesson in determination and how not to give in to defeat. Self-preservation became a top priority. At our store, no one was turned down when asking for "credit" to buy groceries and necessities for the family. This naturally became a very heavy burden for Newton Bros. Store, but they were willing to gamble for the sake of needy people. Sometimes farmers tried to pay part of their bills by bringing us cream, chicken, or perhaps some beef or pork if they had butchered a cow or pig. Countless people were never able to pay their bills.

At about this time, we found ourselves going through a terrible drought. We were besieged by droves of grasshoppers that stripped the farmlands of everything that grew. One could not tell that anything had ever been planted or grown there. The corn fields, once green and beautiful, were reduced to a mere stubble. All was bare and desolate. We could do nothing but pray for rain.

In much earlier years, Indians had occupied this land in South Dakota. They shot arrows and used tomahawks for hunting. Many of these were left on the ground. As white men took over and tilled the soil, the Indian tools and relics were covered over. Then came the dust storms. Our homeland became known as the "dust bowl".

The "dirty thirties" we endured were beyond comprehension. Days were like night as the street lights were on all of the time. The air was totally black with dust and everything we touched was gritty and grimy. We went to school in the dark, covering our faces with scarves in order to breathe. In our home it was my job to dust the window sills. I used a dustpan and a whisk broom to clean off over a half-inch of dust every day. Mother dampened sheets and hung them over the doors to stop the dust from seeping in. It penetrated through everything.

On the farms, the dust completely covered fences and outbuildings. One could walk right over the top. In some cases there were patterns of fine soil that looked like the sandy desert. After school, many days we walked the fields searching for arrowheads and other Indian artifacts which had been an important part of this land many years before. It became our "entertainment" as we discovered and collected these treasures.

Survival was not foreign to us in central South Dakota. If we were considered strong and determined it was no coincidence. Life continued, and when things became better we appreciated what we had more than ever before.

6

Social life seemed more important as I became a young lady. I had always played with boys in our back yard and I enjoyed their friendship. I often said they were better and truer friends than girls, although I had a number of close girl friends. By the time I was thirteen, I found myself thinking of boys in a different way. I felt flattered that several boys paid attention to me.

One boy in particular (the only redhead in our school), often looked across at me as we sat opposite each other in orchestra practice. If I glanced at him at the same time, I was aware that I blushed for some unknown reason. Strange that this was the same Gordon that I had known all my life and we had been content playing "pump-pump pull-away" together.

We became braver, and frequently Gordon would ask if he might walk me home from school. He was two grades ahead of me, and by the time he began playing basketball in high school, I thought he was outstanding. When I was fourteen, he gave me a little silver ring (which I later lost) that had belonged to his grandmother.

My mother thought he could do no wrong, and I knew I could always go places with Gordon when he invited me. In turn, his parents, Abie and Mable, approved of me. Once in a while his Dad would let him have the car to take me on a date.

In the meantime, I found other boys attractive. There was one in particular, Ken Glaze, who was the star on the Hitchcock High School basketball team. Because we were twenty miles apart, I only saw him when our two rival teams had a game. Sometimes we would have just a few minutes to talk, but I kept hoping that we could become better acquainted. He had the blackest hair and eyes I had ever seen, and I thought he could easily be a movie star.

I turned fifteen in December and life seemed more exciting every day. I was a romantic and a dreamer, always anticipating the next wonderful event in my life.

March came, and I was shaken to the very depths with the death of my father. I had never known the loss of anyone close to me, nor was I prepared for such a tragic loss. Again, I felt that I must be the strong one for Mother's sake.

The three days that followed seemed a nightmare as people streamed through our house with the open casket at the foot of the winding stairway. I thought if only I could run away, or perhaps awaken to find it was just a bad dream. No one seemed to notice how this affected me, for they were more concerned for my now widowed Mother.

One day I stood in the kitchen feeling lost when Doc's daughter, Maxine, who had been as close as a sister, came into the room. She simply took me in her arms and held me. I shall never forget how comforting it was to know she understood and cared.

The next day my good friend, Gordon, courageously came by and asked me if I would care to go for a ride in the car. It was a wonderful escape, even if only for a short while. I was impressed by his sympathy and thoughtfulness. Curiously, the same day, I received a meaningful sympathy card from my friend, Ken, in Hitchcock. I remember thinking how special these two boys were. I was also mindful of the fact that Gordon would be graduating and leaving soon to begin his college education at the University of Minnesota to become a chemical engineer. Little did I know what a strange twist these happenings would have later in my life.

The next two years passed quickly, and before I knew it, I was graduating from high school. There were nine boys and three girls in my class. Three of us planned to further our education. I was able to go on because Dad had left me a small amount of money, and by working too, I could raise the $500 needed per year for room, board, books and tuition. I decided to attend Huron College to be near home and Mother. I was given a job in the Music Department.

I had planned to major in music, but it did not take long for me to realize I could never become a performer and play before an audience. I was to play in a piano recital and I thought I would die a thousand deaths before that day arrived. I had memorized my piano solo very well but about half-way through it, my mind went totally blank. I stopped and started several times but I could not get over the place that caused the snag. Naturally, I was heart-broken and humiliated to have this dreadful experience before an auditorium full of people. I left the stage to find my piano instructor standing right at the door. She had my music in her hand and said, "Now, look at this thoroughy and see what you are doing wrong." Of course I recognized my mistake immediately. The she turned me around and said, "O.K., now go back out there and do it right." She gave me a gentle push out on stage so I had no choice. I played better than I ever had before, but when I was finished I went back-stage, sat on the steps and sobbed bitterly. The janitor was cleaning and said to me, "Now don't cry anymore 'cause that second piece you played was good." He really made my day for I could not help but laugh. I did change my major to Public School Music, however.

Dorm life was a new adventure. We all complained about the strict rules. We had to "sign in" and "sign out" wherever we went. We could go to the library to study until 8:30 p.m. weeknights. We could also have one weekend night out until 11:00. On school nights lights were out at 10:00 p.m. We had an unreasonable housemother who was suspicious of everything and everybody. We loved tormenting her and secretly wished her wig would blow off.

Our girl's club, the I.O.U.s ("Independent Order of the Unattached") flourished, and because we were a "secret" organization, we were the envy of many. Ironically, we never lacked for dates.

In my senior year, I made a huge decision - to attend the University of South Dakota at Vermillion. The school was larger and very different. Parties had been a rarity before, but at the "U" there were fraternities and sororities. I discovered I had led a very sheltered life.

My first day in Vermillion, my roommate, Puggy, and I walked over to the bookstore and who should I meet but Ken Glaze! I don't know who was more surprised. I learned that he was in his senior year and was majoring in education as I was. We brought each other up to date on what had been happening the past three years and looked forward to seeing each other in our classes.

School was never hum-drum because there were social functions every weekend to which we looked forward. I pledged Alpha Phi and moved into the sorority house. Except for "keeping hours", it was quite different from dorm life. We were to learn the social graces, of course. Hours were much more lenient so we felt privileged and we enjoyed being thought of as mature adults. We were expected to date pledges from fraternities on campus as it was important to the status of our "house". Many of these "blind dates" were painfully dull.

It was compulsory that we attend classes regularly. It was necessary to walk across campus from one building to another, and every day I met Ken coming or going. If we had a few minutes between classes, we dropped by the Co-op Book Store for a "coke" (dutch treat, naturally). Our friendship remained casual until early November when he asked me to his fraternity party (Alpha Tau Omega). I learned later that he owned only one suit of clothes and it had been sent to the cleaners. He could not ask me out until he had enough money to retrieve it! He worked at a small cafe downtown that he called a "greasy spoon". He had stayed out of school one full year and worked so that he could complete his education. I admired him for that.

The day of the party came and it was wonderful. We both floated on air. From that time on, we were together every weekend and if possible, in between. We spent entire evenings at the "Varsity", sipping on a coke while most of the others consumed beer and liquor. We could dance there and it didn't cost anything. By December we were "going steady" and liking it more each day.

February 22 was a holiday for George Washington's birthday. The phone rang and Ken asked if he could come right over. It sounded urgent so I said it would be fine. It was a terrible day, with snow blowing and drifting furiously, and it was bitter cold. I met him at the door and his first words were, "'Get your coat and we'll go for a walk." I said, "You must be crazy - it's storming." His answer was, "Let's just go!" I was baffled but proceeded to put on my coat, cap, mittens and boots. We could hardly see as we made our way through the drifts. Finally, after a long silence, he said, "Now this is serious but I have something to ask you...will you wear my fraternity pin?" I was absolutely shocked, for I had no inkling that he was even thinking in that direction, but it didn't take me long to say, "I'd love to." "Hanging" a pin meant that we were now engaged! I thought surely no one had ever felt that way before. It was glorious. With a "pinning", it was customary for the man's fraternity to serenade the lucky lady and present her "house" with a box of chocolates. How exciting it was when I heard their singing outside my window. I then went downstairs and received the candy for my "sisters". I thought I must be dreaming. Everyone was happy for us and we were ecstatic.

We began making plans for after graduation and decided that we would teach two or three years before we married. Graduation was a real milestone and thrill. We were presented with our "sheepskins" at the ceremony and we felt a fine sense of accomplishment as we marched in our caps and gowns.

Teaching positions were difficult to find, but at last Ken was hired as teacher and coach at Winner, South Dakota, west of the Missouri River. My first job was teaching music and English at Hetland, South Dakota, clear across the state. I remember going five miles out in the country for my personal interview with the President of the School Board. I found him in the barn milking the cows, which he continued while we talked. With a college degree, Ken's salary for nine months was $900.00. Mine was $810.00. We both worked very hard and saved for our future together. My room rent was $15.00 per month and board was $35.00 in a private home.

We rarely saw each other but the letters flew between Winner and Hetland. Once in a while a very brief telephone call was made. We were miserable!!! It seemed we were so very far apart.

Just before school was out, contracts were renewed. I received a call from Ken telling me he had been given a $100.00 raise. His salary would be $1,000.00 per year. Incredible! We immediately set the following June 1st as our wedding day!

I could not wait to buy a piano, cedar chest, and some crystal goblets with my hard-earned savings. I couldn't have chosen more impractical items for our home, but then I had stars in my eyes so it was excusable, I felt. Ken made a down payment on a second-hand (or third-hand) Ford.

June 1st, 1940, arrived and we were married in the Presbyterian church in Huron. It was a small but pretty wedding with family and a few friends. The day was a beautiful one with the temperature soaring to over 100 degrees. We didn't notice. Brunch followed at the Marvin Hughitt Hotel. Afterwards, two couples attending tried to "kidnap" me so that we could not leave, but I escaped and ran down the street, my long dress and veil flying in the wind. I managed to reach our little car to find Ken already there. We hurriedly drove away on our way to Minneapolis for a brief honeymoon. We did not know that my brother had placed a firecracker in the engine that he expected to go off when the engine started. It didn't. Thus, about half-way to Minneapolis we began chugging along. We were oblivious to nearly everything but each other. As we reached the outskirts of the city, we knew we were in trouble, and pulled into a gas station. There we discovered that the "bomb" had shorted a wire. Thankfully, it could be fixed. We laughingly said it would be something to tell our grandchildren.

7

Our life together began in the small town of Rock Valley, Iowa, where Ken played semi-pro baseball and worked part-time in a grocery store. He was considered a star on the team, so it was an exciting part of our lives. Prior to our wedding, Ken had spent a summer at the St. Louis Cardinals' training camp.

I did not know how to cook, but I tried. I even attempted to make a cherry pie, his favorite. I used nearly every dish in the kitchen and had pie crust from one end to the other. The greatest thing about it was that he was brave enough to eat it!

The summer passed quickly and we moved to Winner where Ken taught for a second year. Our first home was in the basement of a mail-carrier's home. We had two small rooms. I used the landlady's washing machine and our partial "bath room" was on the far side of the basement. Our stove was a two-burner hot plate and an electric roaster. It wasn't exactly luxury living but we were happy just being together. I did not know anyone but I did a lot of substitute teaching, so that kept me busy. Ken did some refereeing in small nearby towns to earn a little extra money. I always accompanied him on those trips out in the country for I did not want him to drive alone on those side roads during the winter months. It was many miles between towns and we usually had tons of snow.

It was on Armistice Day, 1940, that we had the worst blizzard in years. Our parents, his father and mother and my mother, had come for their first visit. Naturally, I was a bit nervous and wanted everything to be perfect. They arrived safely, but then came the storm and we simply could not get out of the house for three days. The drifts were so high that our little basement windows were completely covered, making our apartment pitch dark. Fortunately, we had enough food so we had a very good time even in "cramped quarters". Their extended visit gave us a chance to become what you might say, "well-acquainted".

As soon as school was out in the spring, we returned to Rock Valley for another summer of baseball. We looked forward to seeing our friends and "fans" again. About the time we arrived, I began having strange spells of not feeling well. I had never felt that way before, and finally I went to a doctor. Lo and behold, we were given the wonderful news that we were to become parents!

Ken had received a teaching and coaching position in Redfield, South Dakota, just twenty-five miles from his home town, and close to mine. We had felt very far away from home so we jumped at the chance. There was no hospital in the town so we planned that we would find a doctor in Aberdeen, South Dakota (forty miles away), and I would have the baby there.

We made friends with another teacher-couple there and were entertaining them at Sunday dinner in our apartment, December 7th, when the news came over the radio - PEARL HARBOR! We had been attacked by the Japanese and we were at war. Because we were at a vulnerable age, we knew that more than likely, it would soon touch us personally.

January came and went. My doctor decided that if nature did not take its course, we would set February 7th for me to be admitted to the hospital. Our winter was frightful, so cold and snowy, and we worried about driving forty miles in such weather. The weather did not let up and February 7th was the start of Ken's basketball tournament!

We drove to Aberdeen that day in a raging blizzard. Ken had to return to Redfield immediately so that he could coach his team. There I was - alone and terrified. He telephoned frequently to check on my progress and paced the floor forty miles away. He arrived the next morning just in time for the birth of our six-pound four-ounce baby daughter, Sharee Lynne. We both felt that surely no one had ever before accomplished such a marvelous feat. After ten days, only being allowed to dangle my feet from the edge of the bed, we departed for Redfield to begin our new life as a family.

Ken had earlier applied for a coaching and teaching position at Washington High School in Sioux Falls, South Dakota. In late summer he received word that they would like for him to report for work there in the fall.

We moved to Sioux Falls where life moved on rhythmically for two years. We were very happy. One day he came home with the news that the "draft" was beginning to call teachers who had been deferred. The inevitable was happening. After some discussion, the decision was made. He applied for admission to Midshipman's School with the U. S. Navy. He was accepted and left promptly for Northwestern University in Chicago for intensive officer's training. Families were not permitted to go because they would be a distraction. I moved to Huron to be near friends who were also "war widows" for the duration. It was a sort of "marking time" place.

Our lives were disrupted, but I was determined to "rise above" the obstacles. Ken had a job to do for his country and I had one of a different nature. I knew I must maintain stability in making a home for myself and our little two-year-old daughter. One of my first decisions was to sell our old car, for gasoline was rationed and it was impossible to go any place. Besides, money was more scarce than ever. I did save enough to travel by train to Chicago to attend Ken's graduation from Midshipman's School. It was a time of mixed emotions for I realized that now we could expect a longer and more difficult separation because of the uncertainty of war. However, it was a proud moment to attend the impressive ceremony. He looked absolutely smashing in his officer's uniform.

The glamour of it all vanished rapidly as Ken received orders to report to the amphibious training base at Coronado, California. He left immediately. I had stayed with friends but it was time to get down to the serious business of finding living quarters. It was next to impossible to find places to rent, but finally one was located. It was one room in a funeral parlor! The double door off the hallway into our room was closed off only by a heavy curtain. I had to carry water from the partial bathroom down the hall for washing and cooking, and waste water back to empty it in the stool. Cooking was done on our little hot plate. Toilet training a two-year-old with the only bathroom facility down a long hall took a bit of doing. Our first Christmas alone was spent in this place. Sharee was at an age that I wished it were possible for her father to enjoy. She missed him, too. I tried to make it as happy as possible. She was the joy of my life.

I learned that many officers were being assigned to duty aboard ship and none of the wives had any idea of the length of time before they would see their husbands. Women and children were advised not to travel, for trains were crowded with servicemen going and coming. After several months, I made a decision. I was going to take my little girl and we were going to San Diego to be with Ken as long as possible. I was warned that he would have very limited free time, but I was willing to take the chance. We boarded a train knowing that it would be three days and two nights before we would reach our destination. We were crammed into a coach that I wasn't a bit surprised to find filled with women (and children) traveling to join their husbands! We struggled with crying children all the way, but the most unbearable part was when we arrived at high altitude and every child became sick. One would have to have been there to appreciate how it was the rest of the way in a closed coach. Mothers took turns trying to get to the wash room to rinse things out the best we could. It was ghastly!

Ken had said there would be no way he could let me know if he could meet me. All I knew was that I had a reservation at the Pickwick Hotel. I did not dare think about being a country girl in a strange city with a small child. When our train pulled into San Diego, there he was to meet me! I was never so glad to see anyone in my life. Then I was given the good news that time in any hotel was no more than three days. I began searching for a place for us but soon found that there simply weren't places for people with children. Instead of "No Pets" signs, there were "No Children" signs. I even called the Salvation Army but no help was available. In the meantime, whenever we saw Ken, we did not know if he would be "shipped out" without warning before we could be together. It was an anxious and trying time.

One day, carrying Sharee (she was so tiny and became so tired of walking everywhere), I boarded a bus going way out on Pacific Boulevard where someone said there were new motels going up and they might serve our purpose. I had never heard of motels, but I persevered and found my way. Sharee and I got off the bus out in the country where these places were all along the highway. I went to several before I found a one room vacancy. We could even stay as long as we wished. I was elated. I paid a deposit and we hopped a bus back downtown. After quickly packing, I left a note at the hotel desk telling Ken the address where we would be staying and left for our new "temporary home". Imagine his amazement when he returned to the hotel and found that we were in a new location! What a joy it was to have a hot plate to warm food for Sharee and a small refrigerator for her milk. I became acquainted with other wives there and we spent some of our "waiting out" time together. We shared a small portable oven that we could use on top of our hot plate so that we did not have to exist on totally fried foods. We just scraped off the blackened parts and thought it was quite elegant. Milk bottles then were round. I even used one as a rolling pin to make a pie. We lived this way for three months, having only an occasional day to take the ferry over to Coronado to the beach or to go to the San Diego Zoo. My shopping was done at the commissary clear across the city - again a trip by bus and with a small child.

At the end of three months, the word came that Ken was to report to Long Beach where he would be assigned to the U.S.S. Butte. I had been preparing myself all along, I thought, for that moment. However, when the time came, I felt as though our plans and dreams were all in crisis.

My little girl and I left California pondering what our future would bring. The trip to Huron, South Dakota, was a bleak one, especially when our Thanksgiving dinner consisted of a bologna sandwich smuggled to us by a service man who had a small daughter at home. We were not allowed at the snack bar.

We set out to pick up the pieces and be on our way. Newton Bros. Store had been sold due to good roads leading to Huron where people could shop. Mother had sold our home in Wolsey and it was moved into the country. I began once more looking for a more suitable place to live. Friends told me of a vacant house within walking distance of shopping that might be available. By this time we were into the dead of winter which made it more difficult to get places on foot. I located the landlord and proceeded to rent the house. He was not knowledgeable about preparing an empty two-story house for winter, so when we moved in and started a fire in the coal furnace, the water pipes in the bathroom upstairs burst and the entire dining room ceiling came down, with water and plaster everywhere! It was discouraging, to say the least, but I called the landlord and fortunately he could get someone to come to our rescue. Soon we were back in business. The next day, I thought the house would be much warmer if I could remove the window screens and replace them with the storm windows in the garage. No stepladder was available but I had a kitchen step-stool so I thought by standing on that I could reach the downstairs windows. With so much snow on the ground and wet boots, it was a chore to find a level place for the stool and especially to keep from falling off because it was so slippery. I attacked the very last window feeling a real sense of accomplishment. Perhaps one more tap with the hammer would complete the job, when WHAM - the hammer went through the window!

To make matters worse, there were everyday problems that confronted me as they did scores of other women who were "making it alone". With no automobile, Sharee and I walked to and from the store, carrying our groceries. Some foods such as sugar and butter and other staples were rationed. We were allotted coupons depending on the size of our family. Many times it was quite sparse by the end of the month. One could not afford baby sitters very often, so social life was confined to gathering with other women and children. We shared news of our husbands and discussed how to handle difficulties with the children. Life was commonplace and certainly not very stimulating. In fact, it was lonely.

Ken wrote a letter every day, but sometimes it would be three weeks before I would hear from him. Then I might receive a packet of letters tied together. They had probably been water-soaked, because of going through typhoons at sea, and barely any part was legible. Mail was censored so we had to be extremely cautious of news we exchanged. We had earlier worked out a code so that when he asked about Mary, I knew that he was in Manila. The most frightening news was when he wrote about expecting to meet Oscar, I knew that he would be at Okinawa. He was there for the invasion. Now, as my mind runs back over these times, it seems like a three-year long nightmare. Surely such stress takes a toll on any human being. It may manifest itself in various ways at a later date. I am convinced of this.

We heard the news that the war was over, almost in disbelief. It had become such a way of life that I'm sure we all had resigned ourselves to accept things as they were. When the celebrating, the bell-ringing and the shouting came to an end, we sat back and waited for the day when we could welcome home our weary husbands. V-Day was a day that left an indelible imprint on my memory.

8

Mixed emotions ran rampant as families attempted to rebuild their lives after the long siege of war. Happiness for those of us who were fortunate to have our loved ones return was intermingled with compassion and sympathy for those who did not have that opportunity. For us, it was a feeling of exhilaration to be together again and get on with our lives.

Ken's homecoming was a joyous occasion, especially for him to be once more with the little daughter he adored and had missed for such a long time. We had not been notified that February 26, 1946, was the date of his honorable discharge, so we did not know when to expect him. That afternoon, Sharee was not about to nap but I did convince her to lie on the living room sofa and look at a book. As she lay there, she suddenly jumped up and said, "Mother come quick! There's a car in front of our house and an Ensign's getting out!" All she knew of an Ensign was a picture she had seen of her Daddy in uniform. Needless to say, we did not lose any time reaching the door. There was a mixture of laughter and tears. He gave us the news that he had been promoted to Lieutenant.

Ken had been advised that his position at Washington High School would be open for him on his return. so we left soon for Sioux Falls to finish out the school year. Shortly after settling into the routine again, he became extremely ill with giant hives - internally and externally. Tranquilizers of various kinds, such as valium and librium, were rather loosely prescribed. He was advised to take them as he felt the need. Physicians said the cause was "just nerves". I learned that this was not the first time he had suffered from this condition. I accepted that perhaps it could be attributed to another radical adjustment in his life and the trauma he had endured. He remained on tranquilizers from time to time for many years. I did not fully appreciate the significance of this problem until much later.

My husband was an individual who never quite felt the compulsion to strive for bettering himself in his work. I recognized early on the potential he had, for he was intelligent and capable. Whenever he had made a change, it was always an advancement. It pleased him when he proved himself and enjoyed success. He liked all types of people and had a special rapport with young people and children. He had patience. Therefore he was an excellent teacher.

With his interest and love of sports, Ken's real desire was to continue his education and specialize in that field. He chose to resign from teaching in order to attend the University of Iowa and work toward a Master's degree. We had made arrangements, including housing on campus, when his parents asked if we would be willing to come to Hitchcock for several weeks to tend their store. They wished to take a much-needed vacation. We agreed. It was a well-named "variety store" for at the front was a soda fountain, to one side "over the counter" medicines and sundries, also cosmetics and many gift items. At the back was the hardware and farm supply department. The day proved to be hilarious when a customer asked for "glycerine sticks" and we searched for them in the hardware!

We were within a few days of Ken's parents' return, when a call came that "Pops" (our nickname for his father) had had a stroke in St. Louis, Missouri. I knew that Ken's place was there. He took the next train. That left me alone to "mind the store". With the help of many kind and understanding people, I managed. "Pops" condition worsened and he was brought by ambulance to Huron, South Dakota, where, after six weeks, the end came.

I had then lost my father, my grandparents, and now my good friend and father-in-law. I remember him for his kindness and his even coolness in a crisis. There was no doctor in Hitchcock so people usually came to "Pops" in an emergency. Everyone loved him. He knew how to manage Ken's mother, who was a good, hard-working woman with a fiery disposition. She would often be short with Sharee and say "No, no - don't touch." "Pops" nearly rolled with laughter when he would say, "Sharee, what does Grandma say?" She would answer, "Bow-wow!" Of course this was something he had taught her. It usually "broke the ice" and Grandma laughed with the rest of us.

Ken was an only child so it was his duty to help his mother make decisions about the future. By this time, school had begun and we cancelled our plans to attend the University of Iowa. If the decision to stay in Hitchcock had been made, we would have lived out our lives in that small inland village of about two hundred fifty people. The thought made me shudder. We both knew that we wanted more than that. We simply could not sacrifice all of our hopes and dreams. Ultimately, the store was sold and we tried to sift out our plans.

I firmly believe in Providence, for so many things happened in my life that showed me the way. When one door closed, another opened. Out of the blue one day came a telephone call from Watertown, South Dakota. It seemed they wanted to find a full-time Recreation Director for the city. Knowing of Ken's athletic prowess and teaching experience, they asked him to come for an interview. It seemed incredible, but we drove to Watertown where he was hired on the spot! It was exciting! Watertown was a fine town of about 15,000 people, located near beautiful Lake Kampeska.

This move was a turning point for us in many ways - a brand new kind of a job, a new community, a new place to live and our little girl would be starting school. Ken's father had left him $3,000 life insurance, so our first step was to make a down payment on a house. We chose a large old house in a pretty residential area of town. It was well-built with solid oak woodwork and the finest materials. The entry hall had a coat closet with a full-length mirror and the doorway opened to another vestibule. It had a winding stairway that led to the second floor. The living room, which would have been called a parlor at the time it was built, was small. There was a sliding double door of oak from the living room to the vestibule. It didn't take me long to realize that it would be a great improvement to remove that whole partition so that lovely stairway would be a part of the living room. It would be more spacious and certainly more attractive. When I approached Ken with the idea, he gave a little shrug and said, "Well, call someone and get an estimate of the cost." I went to the telephone immediately and made an appointment. When the carpenter arrived, he reported that the cost would be $75. It might as well have been $7,500, for it was far too exorbitant for our meager budget. My next question was "Is that a supporting wall?" He said he would go upstairs and check it out. It was not. He was hardly off the porch when I took the hammer and began knocking down plaster and the wall of the partition. Imagine Ken's surprise when he came home for dinner and that wall was down. He accepted it very well after the initial shock. We both knew that we had to then finish what I had started so we pitched in. It was a large task for a couple of novices. We never regretted the change for we loved our home.

Sharee was enrolled in kindergarten and her first day began with her walking to school, hand in hand with the little neighbor boy who was also a beginner. It was the start of a whole new world for her and certainly for us as parents. I choked back a few tears as I watched them until they were out of sight. Our little girl was growing up.

Ken's work was a real challenge - quite different from classroom teaching, but he loved it. He was in charge of all park and recreation activities. This meant he was responsible for organizing everything from sports such as basketball and volleyball teams, ceramic and craft classes, and square and folk dancing, all of which took place in the city auditorium or schools. In winter he directed the flooding and maintenance of ice-skating rinks in all of the parks. In the summer, he supervised swimming and lifesaving classes. It was necessary to transport the children to the lake by bus for this activity as Watertown had no swimming pool. This was a great responsibility for safety reasons. Some days the lake would be rough and it was a risk. There were varied park programs in the summer for all ages. The square dancing and folk dancing we taught together. Thankfully, the minister of our church had been trained in this art and he willingly helped us learn. Ken was the "caller" and I tended the record player. When it was necessary to "demonstrate" a step, we did it. I tried to be a helpmate in any way possible. At the close of our first year, we were invited to the community banquet given by the Chamber of Commerce. I nearly burst with pride when they called his name to come forward. He was presented with a plaque which read, "Kenneth Glaze was recipient of the Distinguished Service Award for outstanding community service during the calendar year of 1948. Through his loyal, faithful, and unselfish efforts he has made a great contribution to his community, state and nation." We were totally overwhelmed.

We became involved in about every facet of the community, always with special interest in our church and schools. We taught Sunday school and had charge of the Junior High Youth group. At one time or other, we held nearly every office in the church. Ken did a lot of officiating at athletic events and I was involved in Music. I continued to compose many numbers for the piano. I called them "diddles" for they were short and expressed how I felt at the moment. One sacred song, "Take Thou My Hand", with words by my sister-in-law, Mildred, I had copyrighted. Nearly all of the others were just memorized and put on tape. It was a satisfying hobby. I played them at several public concerts given by our Music Club. People became aware of Ken's speaking ability so he presided at many public functions as Master of Ceremonies. We were engrossed in community public spirit.

For three years, while City Recreation Director, Ken introduced many well-received innovative programs. When a change in City administration took place, it became impossible to continue these ideas because the new mayor would not cooperate. He said the Recreation program was nothing but glorified baby-sitting. A top priority was a swimming pool, but he got nowhere. Ken knew it was an exercise in futility. Perhaps we were getting a message that we should make a change and leave Watertown. We had been contacted by the Recreation Board in Pittsburgh, Kansas and they seriously wanted him. He went to the telephone to call them to let them know he would accept their offer, when just then our phone rang. He answered and it was the Superintendent of schools saying, "Ken, I realize how tough it is for you to continue on as City Recreation Director, when you are up against a stone wall. Now you people are very important to us in Watertown and we don't want to lose you. What I'm really calling for is to offer you a teaching and coaching position in the city schools." Once more I had to believe that Providence had spared us from leaving. Ken immediately submitted his resignation in order to go back to teaching.

Sharee was now past eight years old and we had been told that perhaps we would never have any more family, although I had even had repair surgery. However, with the strange signals I had been receiving, I wondered if that could be wrong and proceeded to see a doctor. Yes, I was told, we were going to be Mom and Dad again. We were ecstatic! "You must have a boy so Ken will have a baseball player," everyone began saying. The truth was, I felt so miserable for nine months that I just wanted a healthy baby and the sooner the better. Besides, I liked girls. During my pregnancy, I contracted whooping cough from Sharee, so we were a fine pair. I would take two steps up the stairway and begin to whoop. I had to sit up in bed at night in order to sleep. I did not see how I could possibly have a normal baby.

We had been yearning to build our very own little dream house for some months. The only way that could be accomplished was to sell our big house and rent a much smaller place for the interim. It was our good fortune to have a buyer appear just as we learned of a small cottage for rent. We moved just before the baby was due.

One evening, Ken went to a nearby town to participate in a

ballgame with the Watertown Lake Sox. He was gone only a short time when I went into labor. I thought, "How can this be that he is involved in athletics again when I'm about to have a baby? I was reminded of the time before we were married when he jokingly said, "You know, of course, that my first love is baseball." It didn't seem so funny now, however. I remained calm and when he arrived home after 1:00 a.m., he found me getting ready for a trip to the hospital Mother had come to be with Sharee, so off we went. At 9:00 a.m. August 25th, our second little girl made her appearance. We were overjoyed! Some said, "Too bad it wasn't a boy," but Ken said, "No way, for I'd rather have cheerleaders." He never had any regrets for he adored his two daughters. Sharee wanted to name her little sister "Mitzi" so Mitzi Rae became a very special member of our household. Here we were again, a different house, a different part of town, a different job, and a new addition to our family. It was never dull.

That summer, Ken's baseball team won the State Amateur Championship, so he made the trip with them to Battle Creek, Michigan, for the National Tourney. It was very exciting as all the games were broadcast. When they went into the finals the whole town was agog. We could hardly believe the news when they won the National and became the 1950 Champions! A very special bat autographed by each person on the team was placed in the Hall of Fame at Cooperstown, New York. Ken felt that was a highlight of his baseball career. When they returned home, everyone turned out for a big welcoming party. The wives were escorted to the edge of town to meet them. Then with our husbands, we were transferred to convertibles for the parade through town. Bells rang, sirens sounded and with the honking of horns, Watertown never had such a celebration. The huge trophy was a treasure. It was displayed at the banquet that evening. There were many speeches and accolades. Later on, a Baseball Hall of Fame was established at Lake Norden, South Dakota. His bat, used in the championship finals, is permanently a fixture there.

After so many thrilling events that summer of 1950, we were happy to settle down to our usual routine of church activities, P.T.A., school programs, faculty wives, men's faculty, P.E.O., and Rotary. Through all of these groups we made very special friends. One particular group of friends consisted of school board and coaches and wives. It was the usual thing to gather after every football or basketball game for coffee at one of our homes. The men liked to "hash over" the game. Another group was young couples in our Congregational church. We called ourselves the Alden Club. All of us had young families and we got together at the slightest excuse. It was always a fun time. We celebrated birthdays, anniversaries, house-warmings, or whatever we could think of. We also square danced. Many times we dressed in costumes, the more outlandish the better. The women were all noted for their culinary expertise so we ate well. In the fall this group went pheasant hunting together. The smaller youngsters always rode together in Duke's panel truck. To them this was the ultimate. Duke was a bachelor who loved kids and they all loved him. We never failed to take quantities of food for our picnic lunch. That time of year was beautiful and it was great to be outdoors. The youngsters loved it too, especially climbing haystacks. We kept looking for just the right place for lunch, but usually we waited so long that everyone felt starved and we ended up eating in a pasture where there wasn't a tree in sight. We didn't mind, for we had such a good time.

It was on one of those hunting trips that the unexpected happened. Ken had never hunted until we moved to Watertown, so he was rather inexperienced. Some of the fellows left a space between them and walked the cornfields to "scare up" the birds. Others were posted at the end of the field to shoot as the birds came over. It was decided that Ken would be stationed at the end to give him a chance to shoot. The walkers came through and suddenly a whole flock of pheasants flew up. Ken raised his gun, aimed, and "plop", a big rooster pheasant fell right at his feet! He hadn't even fired a shell. The bird had hit a telephone wire and dropped dead right there. We all wished for a camera to capture the look on Ken's face, of course, but he thought it was hilarious, too.

9

Teaching was very important to Ken because of his love for children and young people. However, he began to realize that he could not grow any more in teaching unless he went into administration, and that was not what he wished to do. It was obviously a "tight squeeze" salary-wise for a family man to be a teacher. The thing that seriously made him think about a change was again an unexpected turn of events. An officer from the home office of Midland National Life Insurance Company,located in Watertown, called and asked him to stop by. Ken was dumbfounded when the man said, "Have you ever thought about going into Management of Insurance?" Ken was, of course, so taken by surprise that it took him a minute to answer. He said, "'Good heavens, it never entered my mind." A lengthy discussion followed and he was told that they would be interested in him if he cared to pursue it. He was to let them know within a week. Naturally, when he gave me the news, we were in a state of shock. Office work would be so very different from anything he had ever done and he would miss his students. However, with the promise of advancements, salary, and still a chance to participate in school and community programs evenings and weekends, it was enticing and too great an opportunity to pass up. So, he accepted the offer.

The challenge proved to be great, having begun as Secretary of Agencies. There was much to learn but with Ken's pleasing personality and his aptitude with figures and business, he progressed rapidly. A part of his work consisted of pre-arranging for Midland annual conventions. These affairs included wives. We were thrilled to be able to travel to places that perhaps we never would have seen otherwise. Each year we went to cities such as Montreal, Phoenix, Coronado, New York, Las Vegas, and Mexico City. I even went to the meeting in Mexico in a wheelchair for I had just been released from the hospital with a slipped disc in my back. I wasn't about to miss anything, and besides it was my duty to act as an official hostess at these conventions.

In the meantime, we had found a house plan that we thought was affordable and just right for our little family. The lot we chose was on the northwest edge of town. People said we'd be living "way out in the country" but we especially liked the view and it was within a block of an elementary school. It was exciting to move ahead on such a new venture. Plans were drawn up and the building began. Ours was the only house on our side of the street. The lot was so low that load after load of dirt had to be brought in. Fortunately, the city was cutting down some streets so there was a surplus of dirt that they were glad to haul and dump on our lot. We used a wheelbarrow and moved every bit of the fill ourselves until we had a level lot. Ken kept reminding me of how good we would feel once our mission was accomplished. We did feel good even as we sat with a heating pad at our backs!

The house was completed and we moved in during the summer of 1953. In a short time we had wonderful neighbors with children on both sides of us and around us. It was a special neighborhood where we shared coffee parties, children's activities, croquet under lights in the back yard and lots of picnics. We decided that we wanted to be there forever.

Mother was always available whenever one of her children needed help. Perhaps it was because she knew she had been dependent on us so long. She must have been pleased when we called on her. Frederic's first child, Stanton, had labeled her "Nanna" when he was small and couldn't say "Grandma", so "Nanna" she became to the other grandchildren, Sharee, Mitzi, and Barbara, Frederic's daughter. In fact, she was "Nanna" to nearly all who knew her. She gravitated to children and was a weaver of tales, so they were always content when left with her. She was a true lady who was also lots of fun. Nanna was widowed very young and the family teased her about finding a good man in her life. Her answer always was "I'd only be interested if he was old, had a bad cough, and lots of money." Then she and all of us had a good laugh. She was interested in people of all ages, and she had a keen mind and a love of life. Everyone enjoyed her unique musical talent. With "Nanna", her family was the ultimate. She thought of her daughter-in-law as another daughter, and Mildred was the only sister I ever knew. Surely "real sisters" could never have been closer. This was true too of Frederic and Ken. They were special to each other. Ken had been an only child and he had never known the joy of having brothers and sisters.

Frederic's family lived in Huron, South Dakota, so we visited back and forth frequently and shared holidays and special times. Our girls always wished for lots of folks to be there for it meant more fun. Mildred's brother and family, including her parents, usually joined us for such memorable occasions. Her father, "Uncle Adolph" to the young fry, was a born entertainer. His wooden ventriloquist doll, "Arthur-Itis", that he had made, was always a winner. He very cleverly manipulated Arthur and the kids were entranced. He also played on a saw with a violin bow. They all thought he was fantastic. He was, too.

Ken was doing very well at Midland, Mitzi was about to begin kindergarten, and our family was extremely happy when in July we received a call from Huron that my dear brother, Frederic, had died of a heart attack. At his age, forty-three, one does not expect that kind of news. The memory of that call still haunts me. It seemed impossible. We would never feel the same again. He was a wonderful family man and we all missed him. We felt a great sense of loss but we were a close family and we would carry on.

Sharee and Mitzi began school in the fall and we were immersed in their activities as well as our own. I began giving private piano lessons to beginners and intermediates at the request of neighbors and friends. It was a busy life.

Time passed swiftly. We continued to enjoy our home and friends. We were actively involved with family, church and school. I had no aspirations to pursue a career after teaching for I was happy being a mother and a helpmate to my husband. I loved my home and the care of it as well as the cooking and baking of favorite foods. In summer I canned several hundred quarts of fruit, vegetables, chicken and even pheasant in the fall. After we purchased a freezer, it was stocked full of baked goods and casseroles "in case someone would drop in." We always had a garden and nothing ever went to waste.

It seemed such a short time when suddenly we had a sweet girl graduate. Sharee would soon leave home and go away to school. We were very proud of her, but I'm sure every parent is apprehensive when a child, especially a girl, is on her own for the first time. She had no desire for a large school, nor did she think she should be too close to home, so she selected Drake University at Des Moines, Iowa. We drove to Des Moines that fall and dropped her off at the dorm. She knew no one. That picture always stayed with me as we drove away with her waving goodbye. I'm sure we were the sad ones rather than Sharee. When we returned home, we telephoned her and she was already in the swing of things with a group of girls. They were anticipating the beginning of "Rush Week" the following day. We lived for her letters and the news about school.

Sharee immediately pledged Alpha Phi, her mother's sorority, and social life became a whirl for her, even though she was conscientious about her studies. She mentioned meeting and dating a number of boys, but then there was a change and we were just hearing about Alan, this wonderful senior boy. We attended Homecoming, and of course there was Alan! We fully approved from what we knew of him, but it did seem that our little girl was certainly swept off her feet. That concerned us for we felt she was so young and just getting started in life. He would graduate in the spring.

We attended graduation and were not surprised to find that love was in bloom between the two. Al had been in Air Force ROTC so it was thrilling to watch Sharee pin his wings on his uniform. He was commissioned and was to report to the base at Waco, Texas.

Sharee returned to school in the fall but her heart wasn't in it. We went to visit her and she said to her father, "Daddy, Al and I want to get married." We both turned a little pale, and his reply was, "Sharee, we want you to finish school first. You're too young." With that, we couldn't believe our eyes, for Sharee had always complied with our wishes. She suddenly burst into tears, and sobbing uncontrollably, she said, "But Daddy, we are both just miserable." We knew that it must be so, so her father said very quietly, "Golly, if it's that bad, you have our blessing." She threw her arms around us and of course we all shed a few tears. The reality of it was that our little girl was now a grown woman and she had made a choice about her life.

Mitzi was all excited with the news that she would finally have a brother. She thought he was handsome and "cool." She was involved in the wedding plans with all of us and she was more than pleased when Sharee asked her to be her junior bridesmaid. The date was set - February 17th, 1962. The wedding would be in our Congregational Church in Watertown. Arrangements were made amid a hub-bub of showers and parties plus all the excitement. Sharee's attendants were to be Mitzi, cousin Barbara, and two sorority sisters from Drake. Al's attendants would be four fraternity brothers from Drake. Several others from school planned to come also.

We set up a "dormitory arrangement" in our basement for all the girls and rented rooms at a motel for the boys. They were to have their meals with us. Everything was well planned even though we knew it would be crowded with wall-to-wall people. My only regret is that we did not take pictures of that girl's "dorm". Suitcases were opened and spread all over, the ironing board and iron were in the middle of the room, hair dryers were everywhere, and clothes were hung from every hook, exposed water pipe, or any other place possible. It looked like a tornado had just gone through. But such fun had never occurred in that basement before or ever again.

The appointed day arrived. The out-of-town guests had driven in the previous evening. When we arose the morning of the 17th, there was such a blizzard and so much snow on the ground that we wondered if we could even get to the church. Fortunately, we made it. We were having the reception at the church following the ceremony, with a private supper for family at Midland, across the street, after that. Having never had charge of such a function on a large scale, with so many things that were my responsibility, I couldn't even remember walking down the aisle. I must have floated down. It had been exhausting but worth every bit. The wedding was beautiful. Sharee and Al stayed for the supper afterwards, opening some of their gifts before they left. When all was said and done, and the newlyweds had gone, we loaded our car with all the items and "leftovers" that needed to be taken back to our house. I had such mixed emotions and yet I couldn't wait to get home and kick off my shoes. Friends helped us carry things and wade through the drifts. I opened the door, about to collapse, when I saw a beautiful bouquet of flowers on the table. I thought surely it must be a mistake. I opened the card which read, "Mom, SO glad it was a girl. Love, Al." I was so touched that I sat right down and cried, both from weariness and joy, for I knew that our daughter was in good hands.

That evening after all was calm and the chatter and talk of the wedding ceased, we all fell into our beds. There was much concern about the weather and the several carloads from Drake that would be returning to Des Moines the next day. Rightly so, for the next morning, nothing was moving. All roads were closed in all directions. Fortunately we had plenty of food in our house. I thought, "Oh, my word, we were so happy to have all of these folks come, but how long might they be staying?" My sister-in-law, Mildred, never moved out of the kitchen. She made mountain-sized stacks of pancakes, trying to fill up all of those hungry students. We laughed until we cried, and they all said they had never had such a good time.

These young folks had made the trip to Watertown in light-weight clothing, never worrying about the possibility of bad weather. When the news came that one route to Des Moines was open, I went to every neighbor, gathering caps, heavy jackets, boots and mittens for them to borrow to wear back to Drake. One of the girls helped me prepare boxes of food - leftover sandwiches, cake and goodies from the wedding so that each car would be prepared if it became stalled. The house was so full of people that the only place for us to do this was under the dining room table. We spread a tablecloth down and she and I worked while onlookers were in hysterics. All in all, it was a wedding to remember!

10

It is a curious feeling when one child leaves the nest permanently. It is difficult to "let go". We still had Mitzi at home, thankfully, and now she would receive our undivided attention, which I admit may have been a bit overdone at times. We were vitally interested in her activities and extremely proud of her accomplishments. We also knew that she loved her independence. She reached out to friends who were troubled and could not confide in their parents. Many of them came to our house where they knew they were welcome. Mitzi had an unusual understanding and compassion for people.

Ken continually advanced from one office position to another. He always seemed satisfied although he kept on being plagued with the problem that had been diagnosed as "just nerves". Bottles of valium and librium were always on the window sill in the kitchen for "when he felt the need". There was never a question when he'd call in for refills, so I had no doubts about his medication.

Sharee and Al were living on base in Waco, Texas. It was an entirely new lifestyle for them. She had continued her education for a time at the branch of Baylor University in that city.

Ken was celebrating his birthday that summer when he received a birthday card which read, "Happy Birthday, Grandpa". It took us but a few minutes to understand the message - "We were going to be grandparents!" Unbelievable but wonderful! I'm sure that every mother must feel as I did - surely my daughter could not possibly have a baby without me being there. The time flew and then came the call, January 22nd, 1964. The baby had arrived without me. We had a granddaughter, Jody Lynne. I left immediately by plane, my first trip by air, and that in itself was exciting. It was a bumpy flight, traveling through a severe electrical storm, but I was undaunted for it was only thrilling to be going to visit our first grandchild. Indeed, Jody was a little princess. When she came home from the hospital, everything was in readiness. I suggested that her crib be moved into my room while I was there so that Sharee wouldn't be disturbed. Every night Jody awakened at 2:00 a.m.

for a feeding. I quickly jumped out of bed and warmed her bottle. Half asleep it was pure joy to sit up in bed and give her the bottle as I held her in my arms. She then slept for the rest of the night. I felt like such a noble grandmother to help in that way. My stay lasted ten days and the first night after I'd gone, Sharee decided that when she heard the little "eh eh" sounds, she would wait a bit. Lo and behold, Jody went back to sleep without any further ado. Never again did she have a bottle at that time of night. When I learned of this, I was thoroughly dismayed. I knew that I hadn't been necessary at all. What a shock!

Ken was constantly involved with civic functions and business in the community. He became President of the school board at the time that a new high school and arena was built. It was a proud moment when the dedication took place. Shortly after, an indoor swimming pool was added. At last it was a dream come true. He became very influential in procuring a new vocational-technical school that was a real boon to the community for we had no college there. He made numerous trips to the capitol in Pierre, South Dakota, to promote this project. He was a true, loyal, hard-working citizen. He was by this time Administrative Vice President of Midland, and he was appointed to serve on the Advisory Council for the School of Business at the University of South Dakota.

High school graduation time came for Mitzi. She chose St. Cloud State at St. Cloud, Minnesota. It was hard to believe that our baby was a young lady about to leave us. We now would surely have an empty nest syndrome. She began in the fall and had the experience of going through Rush Week. She, too, made the decision to pledge Alpha Phi. Naturally I was more than pleased to have two Alpha Phi daughters.

Now that Ken and I were alone, I began observing more peculiar things about his behavior. It seemed that we hardly had any communication and he became rather passive. I would sometimes be baffled by this change and would go for long walks at night, trying to collect my thoughts. I wondered, "am I imagining things or is something perhaps wrong with me?" It was disconcerting, for no one else seemed to notice. I insisted on regular physical examinations but he was always given a clean bill of health.

Mitzi changed schools and took her second year at the University of South Dakota. She seemed to be searching for something and yet she was undecided about her future. Word came that applications were being taken from the United Council of

Churches for young people to participate in a summer program for underprivileged children. She chose to try for it. She was amazed to hear promptly that she would spend the summer in Birmingham, England. She was to meet seven other students from the United States in New York and have three days of orientation before departure. We drove her to New York City and registered at the designated hotel. It was on the edge of Harlem and about as "non-deluxe" as could be. We even had a rat in our room when we arrived. This location was purposely selected to test these young people with some of the situations that would confront them. It was very difficult to leave her knowing that we would not see our nineteen-year-old daughter for some time. She would be with strangers in a strange land. The other students assigned to her program were from several other countries. Not one of them spoke English. She fell in love with England and especially the children in her group. They had never gone swimming, played in parks, gone to the zoo, and things that so many children take for granted. She had a fantastic summer and reluctantly returned home.

Sharee and Al were now out of the service and moved to Albert Lea, Minnesota. They were anticipating the arrival of their second child. On December 5, 1966, Mark Alan was born. We were ecstatic to finally have a boy in our family. He was indeed special. We had kept Jody with us for a few days and I'll long remember when we met Sharee and Al to return their little girl. They had brought baby Mark in a clothes basket. Such a precious bundle!

In the meantime, I was more puzzled each day for Ken was not himself. He still managed all of our financial affairs and paid all bills. I never owned a checkbook. He told me nothing of business. Mitzi was in her third year at the University of South Dakota. Neither of our daughters were with us enough to notice the subtle changes in their father. The bottles of tranquilizers were still on the window sill.

Mitzi had a strong desire to go back to England, hopefully to find work there. We told her that she must pay her own way, so she worked until she had enough money to take her there. She lived a very frugal life, cleaning apartment buildings, and other types of work that were totally new to her. She was determined as usual and finally became a probation officer in the city of Birmingham. Her experiences were unbelievable for a girl of her age. One of her duties was to chaperone young girls who had perhaps begun prostituting by the time they were eleven years of age. It was a way of life for them and they saw nothing wrong with it. Prostitution in England was not illegal. Soliciting was. She had to make sure they were not on the streets by themselves. They had already had previous arrests.

It was during this time period in her life that Mitzi met John, who would later become her husband. We could tell by the tone of her letters that it was something we could expect. He was a classical musician, born and raised in England. We, of course, had concern about whether she would ever return home to stay.

In reflecting back, many times we see mistakes we made unknowingly with our children. We try to use our best judgment for we want what is best for them. Sometimes the road we take may have a turn that we do not expect and we have regrets. This we cannot change and must accept. Mitzi had found romance while she was still in high school, but we thought it was a case of "puppy love". The boy was older and had already finished high school. We had such high hopes and aspirations for her, and she was at such a young age, that we discouraged their being together. She was a free spirit and wanted to experience seeing the world and all of life. It is difficult to know what might have been had that relationship developed into a lasting one. Ken was oblivious to most things so the decisions that were made were generally mine. It was awesome, but I took responsibility. I could not imagine her being content, spending the rest of her life in Watertown without having the chance for adventure. I may have been wrong.

Sharee and the family were by this time in Minneapolis They visited us weekends quite frequently and we in turn visited them. When they came to Watertown it was a beautiful time for several years. I baked for days and we always planned special events. Ken taught the grandchildren to play ball so our yard became a gathering place for all the neighborhood. He was so popular with all the neighbor children that many times they would come to our door and ask, "Can Ken come out and play?" He was a friend to all.

11

Gradually, Sharee and Al began to notice differences in Ken. He offered little in the way of communication and seemed to feel uneasy with family and friends. I found that I was helping him more with routine things every day. It was frustrating and I was often provoked when he could not handle simple tasks. Ken was in line to be President-elect of the Advisory of the University of South Dakota School of Business. I was so proud of him, but at the same time, apprehensive, for I seemed (or so I thought) to be the only one noticing the change in him. We drove to Vermillion South Dakota to a Council meeting, and upon arriving I became ill. I couldn't imagine what was happening, but when I looked in the mirror I found that one whole side of my face was paralyzed. We returned to Watertown immediately to learn that my problem was Bell's palsy. I struggled with this miserable illness for six weeks before I improved and returned to nearly normal. I felt certain that stress played a big part in it. I think I knew in my heart that Ken would never be President of the Advisory - probably would be unable to retain his position on the Council.

At the close of 1969, Ken came home one day and said he had been called into the office. It was "suggested" that he make a change. He had two options, one to assume the duties of a lesser position in the company office, the other, to perhaps leave the office and join one of the agencies to try selling insurance. It was a crushing blow for neither of us understood the reason for such seemingly unfair treatment. There simply was no explanation. No one implied that there had been anything wrong with his performance at the office. For a man of Ken's stature, his impeccable honesty, and the respect of the entire community, this was hard to believe.

I attempted to learn how such a thing could happen, but I could not bring myself to go to the Administration to determine the answer. Ken was, of course, dazed and I was perplexed, but I was also angry. I questioned many things. In desperation, I went to our minister for support. Again I was disillusioned, for even though he said he was sympathetic, I did not feel any reassurance from him. It was as though he was at a loss for words. We never again discussed the issue.

I knew that Ken needed help with making a decision and it was up to me. I felt that he should not have to suffer the humiliation of remaining in the office. One of the General Agents learned that Ken might be considering sales, so he approached him and offered him a job, which he accepted. People so highly regarded his knowledge of the business that they came to him to buy insurance. By the close of the year, he had done well enough to belong to the President's club and was awarded an all-expense trip for us to Switzerland, where the Midland convention was to be held.

We made the trip to beautiful Montreax, Switzerland, in company with other winning agents and their wives. It was unforgettable. While we were in Europe, I decided we should see a bit more than just one country. At the end of the meeting we flew from Geneva to Rome where we spent two days touring all of the places we had only read about previously. It seemed like a dream to actually be there. It was not always easy because Ken became confused at times and I was responsible for all plans. Besides, I was not feeling well. Mitzi was still in England, so the highlight was to go from Rome to London where she and John met us. We then drove to Birmingham for a short stay. It was interesting and at the same time dismaying to see how our daughter lived there, but the thrill of being with her was the best thing that happened in a long time. She had arranged to take a week and travel the continent with us. We had our first experience on a hovercraft when we crossed from Dover, England, to Boulogne, France.

We spent a couple of days in Paris which were fascinating, but it was there that a curious thing took place. One day, as we were having lunch at a sidewalk cafe, Ken suddenly burst out angrily at Mitzi and said, "We have done enough for you. Now it's time we did something for your sister." This episode had no meaning at all and I could see the shock and concern in Mitzi's face. We tried to let it pass as though we didn't hear, but truly, we were both bewildered. I was sure that she, perhaps for the first time, sensed that her father was different from the father she had known.

Mitzi was such a seasoned traveler by this time that it was easy for us from then on. We traveled by train through lovely country and spent several days in Vienna. Mitzi had said it was a "must" and she knew we would love it because everything there was in 3/4 time. It was pure delight.

From Vienna we took the train through the Alps to Zurich to

meet other Midland people for the return home. It was there that we said good-bye to our darling daughter and she went back to England. There were all kinds of mixed emotions from the experiences we'd had, to being with Mitzi, meeting John, and the strange helpless behavior that was apparent in Ken.

Our trip home was uneventful except for missing our flight out of New York, which made us late. When we finally arrived, it was very good to be home.

I made an appointment with our physician and within a few days I was admitted to the hospital for major surgery. This time of my life was extremely critical. I was not too surprised that Ken did not come to be with me. However, before I went into the operating room, there stood Sharee and Al. What a lift it was to see them. Al had brought her to Watertown to spend a few days with me. I was richly blessed. Time has a way of healing and I had strong faith. I looked upon my health as a temporary stumbling block. I felt positive that Ken would work out of his troublesome dilemma and would continue to do well. He did so for several months, then I could see that pressure was affecting him. I attributed it to the kind of work he was doing and the stress of learning something new at this point.

Our only nephew and family lived in Honolulu. They had invited us many times to visit them. I thought perhaps this was the time to have a change of scenery and Ken might return re-energized. We made a most enjoyable trip over. On the flight, they played a guessing game. They asked the passengers to figure out how many miles we were from our destination at that particular time. Ken, having been a navigator aboard ship, missed the correct answer by a fraction. We won a bottle of champagne. We proudly waved our prize as we disembarked from our plane. We were met by our family. It was a constant round of activity while there and we inhaled the beauty around us. We also spent time with our dear friends living there who were with us on that December 7 years before, when Honolulu was attacked. They gave us a tour of Pearl Harbor, which was nostalgic for all of us. Ken did quite well except for one evening when he became extremely ill. We thought perhaps he'd had too much sun that day playing golf.

It was coincidental that on our return home, we had the same flight attendants we'd had going over. They remembered us and we joked and had a good time. About halfway they came to us and gave us two packages. We couldn't imagine what this was all about until we opened the card which read, "You have just been chosen 'passengers of the month'". We were overwhelmed. We received a lovely Hawaiian record and a set of bamboo tumblers. What a fine keepsake!

By the end of that year, Ken was doing less and less business. I learned quickly that with insurance sales, one must sell if there is to be any income. I became paranoid because our home was not fully paid for, we had very little savings, and we weren't going to be able to "hold out" very long.

I took a job as teacher's aide at an elementary school for my teaching certificate had long ago expired. The Recreation Board came to see Ken for they needed a replacement for the present Director. I was elated for I had no doubts but that with my help he could do as he'd done before. Not so - it lasted about two months and sadly he was given the news that perhaps they had made a mistake. My heart sank to the very depths. I continued the struggle, but on some days I had to leave school early because something had gone wrong at home. I felt uneasy every time I'd go any place. I would make appointments for him in hopes he could sell another policy. I helped him with his hat and coat, but he would blankly stare at me, totally bewildered. He simply did not know where to go or what to do. I continued to deny what was happening.

In the meantime, we had to dip into our savings and I had acquired bills of all kinds. I realized we could no longer live in our house. Sharee was apprehensive about us and suggested that if we sold our house, we should perhaps come to Minneapolis where they lived and she might be of help. She was my constant mentor and a real source of strength. Al, too, was very supportive. The house was sold quickly and at a low price in 1974. I nearly gave it away, but I had no time to waste.

I was aware that we could not move to Minneapolis without some kind of financial backing. Sharee had learned that people were needed at a huge new apartment complex near her to serve as assistants to the building managers. I applied and we were hired. We would have a rent-free apartment. It seemed ideal. It was painful to leave our home and friends of so many years in Watertown and go to a strange city where we knew no one except family. The move was expensive, too. By this time, Ken stood by watching, unable to even tie a box.

It was about this time that I heard from my college roommate, Puggy. She lived in the nearby suburb of Burnsville. At least I had one friend! Little did we dream when we graduated together in 1939 and she left for the cities to work, that after many years our friendship would be so important again in 1974. She, of course, had also known Ken so my dilemma was of great concern to her. She was loyal and offered to "be there" for me whenever the going was rough. I had always heard people say "there's no friend like an old friend." I soon came to know its true meaning. We knew each other so well that we could totally confide in each other. She saw me through many dark moments.

Another complex problem entered into the picture because Mother had been living in her own apartment in Watertown. It was necessary for her to be near the family, so I could not move away and leave her behind. Again, Sharee took charge and found a small low-income apartment for her that would be close to us. Consequently, we had two households to move.

Mitzi returned from England for she had been in touch with Sharee and knew that we were faced with a very grave problem. John followed her and a simple but beautiful chapel wedding was planned for family and friends. Sharee, Al, Jody and Mark were the attendants. With my help, Ken and I took Mitzi down the aisle. Ken looked exceptionally handsome and well. I've always been grateful that he could take part in the wedding as he did. A number of our dear friends from Watertown came. It was a happy day. I had no idea of what the future held for us.

We had an attractive apartment where we were to be assistants. The building was not yet finished. I was "on my own" but I was determined to make it work. Within a few days I found that we were not only assistants, but we were caretakers, expected to clean apartments and get them ready for occupancy as soon as possible. As the plasterers and painters moved out, I moved in with my cleaning supplies. I scraped gobs of plaster off of doors, windows, mirrors and fixtures as well as papers that were glued on. I worked until my fingers nearly bled and my nails were broken. I felt totally drained.

In the meantime, as Ken had never had a complete neurological examination, we felt it was a top priority. I was given the diagnosis in a hospital waiting room filled with people. The doctor said, "Your husband has Alzheimer's disease, a progressive, irreversible brain deterioration, for which there is no known cause or cure. That's the way it is. You'll have to go on from there." He excused himself to see another patient. I never saw that doctor again. There was no explanation nor direction as to where I might turn for help. My children were with me and I silently thanked God for each of them. My son-in-law, Al, asked, "Mom, do you feel like a widow?" Numbly, I answered, "I guess I do." Later John inquired of another doctor, "What can I do to get to know this man that everyone loved?" The doctor solemnly answered, "John, you never will." Our sorrow ran deep and our hearts were broken.

I asked the management for a transfer that perhaps I alone could handle. He was kind enough to send us to a smaller complex at a beautiful lake 40 miles from our family. It was a beautiful location, but every week there were parties and I did the cleanup. Laundry rooms were often used as bathrooms, and people became sick in the halls. I knew there had to be a better way. I could not leave Ken alone. I took him by the hand wherever I went.

With the termination of income and with our ongoing expenses, I became desperate. I moved five times in 18 months by necessity. He came with me. We lived in an ever-diminishing world. I was in a strange city and I was not free to find employment. I attempted part-time work - everything from teaching nursery school, tutoring children with special needs, clerking and teaching piano at a keyboard center, but I could not leave for any length of time.

Ken's benefits had all been terminated and I was advised by an attorney not to fight it. It would be too costly for me to pursue it. Our income consisted entirely of his Social Security disability. I had accumulated expenses until there was no reserve. With the 24 hour vigil, I became totally exhausted - physically and emotionally. It became frightening living with this stranger who might push me or twist my arm, or throw things at the television. The loving, gentle husband I once knew was no longer there. He became a shell that simply breathed.

It all seemed unreal and I felt no sense of belonging. Many times there were embarrassments. People usually turned away. This behavior became an obsession with our entire family. I knew that we could not live that way any more. We visited 20 nursing homes in one day and finally found one that would take him. He was admitted the next day. I began feeling tremendous guilt and questioned if I might be "copping out". I wondered how long I could manage the costs for insurance and Medicare did not cover this problem. I was told my car was too new for me to qualify for medical assistance. At the end of three months I received a call that he had become violent and they had moved him to a private hospital in downtown Minneapolis. After six days, his chart was reviewed and they discovered that it read, "This man has no insurance or Medicare (he wasn't old enough). In an emergency call the Veterans Administration." After their call, he was admitted pronto. At the close of the day, I came home to my small apartment, feeling a despair that is impossible to put into words. I was suddenly alone and desolate. I must now begin to really "go on from there."

One of my first assignments was to pass the driver's test, for I would be doing all the driving. I hadn't driven in the city since there was such heavy traffic. I certainly had never driven on the freeways. I studied diligently, and after failing the first test, I made it through. I was petrified every time I'd drive, even to the grocery store. I thought, "I'll never be able to live here and be independent." The first time I drove to the airport and back, I came home and took two tranquilizers and went to bed. I had to grit my teeth, for I knew I must be in control of my life. I told myself, "It's not what happens to you that makes a difference - it's what happens in you."

12

After several weeks of living alone, I decided that there must be families somewhere who were confronted with a similar problem, and if so, I must locate them. Having had several years' experience with Alzheimer's, before the diagnosis, I felt that I might be able to help such families. Surely we could support each other. Paging through the telephone directory, I discovered that the Mental Health Association of Minnesota was located within a few blocks of my apartment. It was a place to start. It was now the year 1977. I went there and introduced myself, briefly telling them my story, and that I was searching for Alzheimer families. They were sympathetic but at that time none had ever heard of Alzheimer's Disease. I finally found one young woman, Karen Peterson, who immediately became interested in my proposal. We spoke of the possibility of organizing support groups for such families, but of course we needed to first find them. We became more excited as we talked of our plans. The first step was to find out if there was already such help available. I made hundreds of phone calls to agencies, hospitals, churches, and other places to inquire. No one knew of any such thing. A friend in my apartment building, Ruth Youngdahl Nelson, suggested we contact Mount Olivet Church to ask if space might be available for meetings. We did, and we were welcomed. We decided on the name REACH, an acronym for Reassurance to Each, and sent brochures to all of the same contacts previously made. The brochure was designed by the M.H.A.M. and the information was directed to families who had a mentally ill or neurologically disabled member. We still were not sure we would ever find any Alzheimer families.

The Minneapolis Star and Tribune called and asked me for an interview. I knew that in order to find others like myself, I must openly and candidly tell my story. I called my plight the "funeral that never ends". A full page was given to this shocking experience with pictures and the headlines containing my quote: "THE FUNERAL THAT NEVER ENDS". The Associated Press picked it up and soon I began hearing from families in other parts of the country. Also, by this time, five other families in Minneapolis had found us. Support groups began springing up. I finally knew that I wasn't the only person in the world with such a bewildering predicament.

It was then that I made the suggestion that perhaps now was the time for us to "spin off" since our needs were different from those of the mentally ill. There was no treatment for our people with Alzheimer's. It was agreed that we incorporate. We would be a separate entity from REACH so that we could do our own funding. Our hope was in research and it would take money. REACH support groups continued on, spreading to other parts of the country.

Again, one morning when I awakened I realized I had Bell's palsy on the other side of my face. One side had been bad enough but now this! I remembered the quote given to me by a dear little elderly friend - she reminded me that it says in the Good Book, "And it shall come to pass" but nowhere does it say, "It shall come to stay."

Hilda Pridgeon, Muriel Erickson and I went to the bank to open a checking account, having to dig into all three of our pockets for the $20 that was necessary. Hilda requested (along with a letter from me) that she be given social service leave from her management position at Control Data. Within 10 days it was granted for one year. They also offered us space for meetings and agreed to print our newsletter. The word began spreading and we grew rapidly. It was almost frightening when we were so long in finding our first few families. We were on our way!

In the meantime, I was guardian for my mother. She was a remarkable person for her age and she always enjoyed our family times together. She was my confidant and best friend. One day I stopped for her to take her to my daughter's for a gathering. As she passed though a heavy door, it bumped her and she fell on the cement floor and crushed her hip. At 92 years of age, this was such a traumatic shock to her that she never recovered. She knew she could never live independently again so she simply chose to die. I realized that my mother was gone and I felt a part of me was gone as well. I had already lost several dear loved ones.

In November of 1978 I was overwhelmed to learn that I was the recipient of the National Mental Health Associations National Volunteer of the Year Award. My entire family was invited to the dinner and presentation. It was exciting. A bit later, I traveled to Washington, D.C. to receive the National Center for Voluntary Action Award, for the REACH program.

In September of 1979, I was invited to attend a Symposium on

Dementia in Minneapolis sponsored by the University of Minnesota and the Veteran's Administration. I wrote to four of the Alzheimer caregivers who had previously been in touch with me and gave them information about the approaching meeting. They were from Seattle, Washington; San Francisco, California; New York City, and Columbus, Ohio. I asked if they would be interested in attending and discussing the possibility of a national association for Alzheimer's disease. They each sent a representative. It was an informative meeting with a number of our Minneapolis families there also.

Marian Emr, assistant to Dr. Robert Butler, director of the National Institute for Aging, attended the meeting and reported the enthusiasm of this group. To our surprise, the next month we were invited to Washington, D.C. by Dr. Butler to discuss the formation of a national association. Several other representatives, one from Boston, MA and another from Pittsburgh, PA, were included in addition to Jerome Stone, an interested family member from Chicago, IL. Several medical professionals observed this session at the N.I.A. The name Alzheimer's Disease and Related Disorders Association was chosen and it was decided to begin incorporating. The date of our first official meeting in December of 1979 was set.

The small group of people met at that time, elected officers, and were off and running. Jerome Stone, the wisest choice we could have made, was elected President. I accepted the appointment as National Program and Chapter Development Chairman, pledged to assist chapters starting up across the nation. My files were already filled with names of families needing assistance. I was also elected to the National Board of Directors. Our goals were established: Family Support, Education, Public Policy, and Research.

I had no idea that day that my life as a volunteer would be so involved and rewarding. I have often used the quote, "In volunteering, it isn't what you give or get, but what you become." That is certainly true. It seemed that because I was a pioneer who really understood any problem they might be encountering, families called upon me for counseling. My expertise was in my experience. I found myself continuing to "educate" both the medical and lay community long after I thought my teaching days were past. I felt the need for more confidence in the area of counseling so I enrolled at the University of Minnesota for a summer. After being out of school for so many years and finding my classmates were the ages of my children, I felt a bit apprehensive. How gratifying it was when

I found I could do it.

In the meantime my telephone rang early and late every day and night. As draining as it was, it became my lifeline. At last I felt I had a purpose. My life became a merry-go-round that was nonstop. A first challenge came about when I was invited to travel to Washington, D.C. to testify before Senator Thomas Eagleton's Committee on behalf of the thousands of our families. It was an awesome responsibility, realizing that if we were to make an impact, it depended on my effectiveness. I had to pinch myself to see if I might be dreaming. My testimony appeared in the July 15, 1980, Congressional Record. I was quoted in publications such as Generations, Discover Magazine, Twin Cities Magazine, IMC Journal, Modern Maturity, Journal of Gerontological Nursing and many newspapers. A short time later, I was invited to participate in a Mini White House Conference, addressing the needs of our people. Requests came from the National Gerontological Association for a presentation as well as appearances at medical schools, universities and veterans hospitals. My suitcase was always ready to go. My only request was that my expenses be paid. I was on a fixed income and I was totally volunteer. I carried and distributed literature wherever I went. Medical journals and other publications began telling the story of the strange word "Alzheimer's" that had previously been an unknown. Our Association continued to mushroom with new chapters and support groups in many states. I was also beginning to have inquiries from other countries. I then realized that Alzheimer's was of universal concern.

What evolved as the result of my counseling and the beautiful people I met, as well as the places I found myself, was incredible. I was not a professional. I was simply a lay person with an abundance of experience. My Alzheimer's "family" continued to grow. I had loving and caring friends everywhere. We had a bond like no other. I urged and encouraged them to become involved in helping others, sharing, directing, and guiding. I had already found it to be extremely therapeutic, for listening to their stories did not allow time to dwell on my own misfortune. When someone thanked me for helping them through a difficult period, I often wondered what I had done. Trusting me because they knew "I had been there" and understood, seemed to be the key. They could not tell me of any problem that shocked me. I "drove" myself constantly, answering personally every letter I received. I made a phone call if it seemed urgent. I was "on call" at any hour.

13

I became immersed in the work I was doing, and what might appear depressing to some, actually stimulated me. It was a gratifying challenge which became an obsession.

I shall never forget an emotional experience that took place in Washington, D.C. at the time of our first organizational meeting. Hilda and I had gone there to join others and make preliminary plans. We had one full day of sharing ideas which we found exhausting and difficult. Everyone had different suggestions. We decided to stay over an extra day in order to meet with Minnesota Congressmen, give them our literature and inform them of our needs. It was extremely warm, and after keeping seven appointments, we hurried to catch our return flight to Minneapolis. We stopped at a snack bar for a cold drink before boarding, but found there was no place to sit. A lovely looking lady, seated alone, motioned for us to come to her table where she invited us to share her booth. I inquired where her destination might be and she answered, "Florida". Then I asked if she lived there. She said rather wistfully that she was there part-time. Then she added, "But I lived in Maine before. I sold my home there when my husband died." I could not help but sense a strange tone of her voice. She went on to ask what brought us to Washington. Our time was limited, and feeling she wouldn't understand, I replied that we were volunteers. "What do you volunteer?" she asked. Having repeated our story seven times before that day, I quickly answered, "We are organizing an Association because our husbands both have a strange malady called Alzheimer's Disease." She grasped our hands and with tears streaming down her face, said, "You may not believe this, but my husband isn't dead. He has Alzheimer's Disease." We stood in silence before we embraced as if we were sisters. It still seems incredible that three of us with the same problem met in the Washington, D.C. airport just minutes before she left for Florida and we left for Minneapolis. She had never spoken to anyone about the disease and had had no guidance or information. We proceeded to give her literature and put her in touch with others from her area. It was beautiful.

There were many true stories that only people who have walked in those shoes would understand. One woman wrote a 14-page letter, pouring out her heart to me, relating incident after incident that I'm sure she felt no one else had ever endured. To me it was like a broken record. At the close of the letter she added, "P. S. Bobbie, I think we were very much in love once, but I can't remember it now."

I recall the telephone call from a woman in Arizona. Her husband had been ill with Alzheimer's for nine years. They had a little dog that was her constant companion and helped alleviate the loneliness as her husband no longer communicated. Her loyal pet slept by the bed every night and only disturbed her if he wanted to go outside. It soon became necessary for the woman to place her husband in a permanent care facility. The day came for her to take him, and upon leaving him, she returned home feeling shallow and empty. It was rather late that Friday evening when she decided to try to get some sleep. The little dog lay beside her as if he understood. When she awakened, she went to the door to bring in the morning paper. Glancing at the date, she was shocked to find that it was not Saturday morning's paper, but instead Sunday morning's paper. She and the little dog had slept through from Friday night until Sunday morning. She became alarmed and telephoned her doctor for an appointment. Upon examining her, he said, "There is nothing wrong with you except that you have slept with one eye open for nine years."

In the beginning, V.A. hospitals were generally reluctant to admit our patients because they were "untreatable." Policies also varied from state to state. A few families were fortunate to have their veteran accepted. The telephone calls and letters I received were heart-breaking for so little was understood of the disease and the effects on the family. Of course, this was true of all hospitals.

One wife whose husband was 48 years old wrote to me about how he had been committed to a state mental institution and they were waiting, hopefully, for a vacancy to occur in the V.A. hospital. There were five children, the youngest of which was seven. It was the Christmas season and she and the children were trying to put the pieces of their lives together, and carry on with family traditions. It was such a hollow feeling and there were many mixed emotions with the grief they were sharing. Yet there was a sense of relief, because the person who had played such an important part in the family and had since become irritable was no longer threatening. It all seemed like a bad dream. She kept reminding the children that they must remember he was ill. Therefore, they should concentrate on the happy times. He was ultimately admitted to a V.A. hospital.

After taking her husband to several V.A. hospitals where there was no room, another woman finally found one that would admit him. She drove home, a 45-minute trip, and as she wearily entered the house, the telephone was ringing. She answered and a voice said her husband did not want to stay there and she should come for him immediately. Upon returning there, she found her husband standing in the street looking completely helpless and bewildered. He had no identification, so it was a real trauma for all concerned. These kinds of mistreatment were many in all kinds of hospitals until a new awareness came about. An interest in learning more about the disease and to understand the desperation of our families became essential. At that time many professionals were "in the dark". Suddenly our families became the experts.

A rather shy and private woman wrote to me of the problems facing her, and I could sense the seriousness of her plight. I was concerned for her welfare for she was near the breaking point. Her neighbors and friends were turning away and she had no one to talk to who would understand. She mentioned the name of her church that she attended so I made a decision to intervene. I telephoned her minister and explained her predicament. I suggested he inform some of those closer to her so that they would realize what was happening and offer her support. This kind of thing became an everyday occurrence.

An elderly man in an eastern state called me every day for a week, pleading for help. He himself was ill and there was no family. He had attempted to place his wife in every care facility in the area and was refused. She was completely unmanageable. He then tried to admit her to a state mental hospital where she was also turned away. So many miles away, and realizing that there was not just one ill person but two, I called the governor's office in that state. It took time and patience, but finally it was possible to break through. In less than a half hour the husband called to tell me his wife would immediately be admitted to a hospital. One would have to experience this to know the gratification that evolved from my work with Alzheimer's families.

There were cases where several in a family were afflicted, and naturally, this created panic. Not knowing if Alzheimer's might be hereditary is a dreadful fear. At this writing there is no proof.

Some caregivers who had been dealing with "around the clock" care for years, became ill and died before the patient. "Letting go" was a real problem because of guilt.

It was not unusual to receive a very late telephone call from someone who pathetically admitted they could no longer stand the strain. Because of our "network" that had been established, putting people in touch with others, it was possible to refer these suicidal caregivers to someone nearby who could offer support and guidance. Sometimes we could make a call to a volunteer who would take immediate action.

There were those who had been refused Social Security disability because of the lack of education about the disease. It was thought that the patient would get better. Not so with this illness. Many people were faced with making several appeals before the problem was solved. I attended several hearings and even gave the judge our literature to read.

There were happy moments for some such as the man in a midwestern city whose wife had been diagnosed three years before. The more he studied and learned about the disease, he became more doubtful and took her for a second opinion - a complete evaluation. Lo and behold, she did not have Alzheimer's, but instead a treatable brain tumor. We all rejoiced with the good news.

Many families were required to "spend down" to poverty level before they could qualify for any financial assistance. It was degrading and demoralizing to have to beg for help, particularly when already mourning the loss of a loved one.

Within one week, three people who knew each other in a small town in Wisconsin learned that they were each dealing with the same disease (A.D.) in their spouses, but they had not been aware of each other's predicament. What a happy thing to know someone who understood exactly and they could share their innermost thoughts and feelings even before support groups came into being.

Hundreds of calls were received asking, "Where should I turn? I am desperate," or I would hear, "If only there were facilities that would understand." One woman said, "the future is so frightening I dare not look ahead." And always the most difficult decision was when it was time to find a care facility, usually a nursing home. The guilt was overpowering.

I could relate a couple of instances that helped me when I found myself in that position. One time was when I finally found a nursing home that agreed to take Ken for two weeks trial basis with the promise that if all went well they would admit him permanently. Our family struggled long and hard with even the thought, but we came to the conclusion that it had to be. I took him in the morning and came for him every day at 4 p.m. He looked well and he seemed to be happy with the arrangement. The afternoon of the last day when I stopped by, they asked me into the office. The supervisor said, "We've decided that it will be impossible to have Ken become a permanent resident for he might wander." I couldn't believe what I was hearing. The family was extremely upset because we had worked hard psyching ourselves up to take this step. As I reflected on what had happened, the thought came to me that it was a blessing in disguise. I had been going through sheer hell, wondering if we were "copping out." Now I had an answer to my prayer. If professionals could not manage his care, surely I couldn't either. It really lifted me up.

Another time, when Ken was later placed in a nursing home, I felt that perhaps I had done the wrong thing. I visited him one day when they came around with cigarettes for those who smoked. He still seemed to enjoy an occasional cigarette so he took one. He must have still been aware enough at that time to realize he did not have a way to light it. (He was not allowed to have a lighter.) Across the room, a woman removed her lighter from her pocket, lit her cigarette and put the lighter back. He noticed her, and without further ado, he stood and walked over to her, put his cigarette in his mouth and stooped over to her. She immediately took the lighter out again, lit his cigarette and put the lighter away. He turned from her and walked back to where I was sitting and proceeded to smoke. It was a complete revelation to me for I had just witnessed two people communicate without speaking a word. It was beautiful. I realized for the first time that he was content with others like himself in a place where nothing was expected of him. If only our families would come to the realization that we are doing what is best for the patient. A good facility can provide necessary care that we are no longer able to give. It is not a cruel step. It is a kindness.

The thing that seemed to haunt a good many was the loneliness. They had enjoyed companionship and a life together for many years, and with this turn of events they found themselves alone. The spirit was broken as their lives continued and their spouses' lives did not. Guilt would not allow them any social pleasures. It was a "Catch-22" situation that was extremely heavy.

14

Time marches on, so they say, and it certainly did in my case as I bounced from one coast to another, meeting families and friends, educating and encouraging them to become involved. I could share some of the do's and don'ts of organizing chapters and support groups, for most were untrained in such matters as I had been. We learn from experience and I had already found plenty of ways to make mistakes. I felt we could all learn from each other. We simply mushroomed and were growing faster than we'd planned and prepared.

By this time my family found that their Mom was a traveling "ambassador" and I seemed to have found my niche. Ken was progressively worse and each time I visited him, I felt ill for a week. I realized that I could not afford for my health to become affected by a situation in which I was at a total loss. I must find ways to turn my thinking around. I decided that I could no longer help him. He was where he had excellent care, therefore I should perhaps direct my energy to helping others. The family rarely went to see him for it became too painful. The grandchildren preferred to remember the fun-loving grandpa who had taught them many wonderful things about life.

One day Sharee and Al announced that their family was being transferred to Florida. It seemed a crushing blow even though I was happy for them. They had been the main reason for my moving to Minneapolis, for Mitzi was still in England at that time. Thankfully, Mitzi and John would still live in Minneapolis even though they were somewhat farther away. Jody and Mark were growing fast and as they were their grandmother's pride and joy I was dreading for them to leave. I wondered again if I should stay in the city, although by this time I had several very special friends who had seen me through many traumas and helped me feel rooted.

My first newly found friend was Fran Thompson. We first met through P.E.O. when I was asked to bring another newcomer to Minneapolis to a reciprocity meeting with me. It so happened that Fran lived within a block of me, and when I called to tell her I'd be happy to stop by for her, I had no idea of what our strong friendship would come to mean. That day, as we were becoming acquainted, REACH was mentioned and she was immediately intrigued by my idea and the fact that it was something that never had been done before. I learned she was a writer, and because of her interest, she began coming to REACH meetings to learn about the families attending and what we were doing to give them support and guidance. Naturally, she began writing stories for newspapers and other publications as well as starting our very own newsletter and also one for the Alzheimer's Association when it began. She was fantastic and a great help to us.

It is curious, how our lives are shaped and how many things along the way are simply meant to be. It was in 1973, while I was still in Watertown, South Dakota, I was reading our P.E.O. Record (our magazine) and came upon a story by a young mother who expressed her deep feelings about her four-year-old daughter, the joy of her life. There was a picture of them hand-in-hand. I turned the page and saw there was a postscript and a picture of them, but now the little girl had grown to womanhood and typically, wore bluejeans and still held her mother's hand. The mother told of her daughter's appreciation for natural wonders, her disinterest in material things and her desire to explore the world and the people in it. It was beautiful.

I was so touched by this story that I cut it out of the magazine and taped it inside my kitchen cupboard. It said so well the same feelings that I had about my young daughter, Mitzi, who at that very time was in England far away, working and helping people and traveling as much as possible. When we moved to Minneapolis the story went with me, and I again taped it inside my kitchen cupboard.

While my mother was in the hospital and we realized she wouldn't be with us very long, Fran, my good friend, was always standing by to give me support. That late afternoon in 1977 mother slipped away and I came home to find a lovely book of original poems and quotes - written by Fran, in my door. Later that evening, as I sat alone, reflecting on what had occurred that day, I opened the book. To my complete amazement, there was the same story with pictures that was taped inside my kitchen cupboard and <u>had</u> been since 1973. It was, of course, Fran's story, and I couldn't believe my eyes. I felt we had been "soul sisters" since 1973, even before we met. Needless to say, we became closer and she continued to be a strength to me in any crisis.

I was invited to Fran's one day for afternoon coffee and met her sister, Carol Bermel, a sculptress, who, too, was interested in the work I was doing. As she inquired about why and what led me to this, Muriel Erickson from across the room, came to me and asked, "Did you say your husband has Alzheimer's disease?" When I answered, "Yes", she said with emotion, "My husband died of Alzheimer's a few years ago." Again, it was providential. I had looked for two years to find someone who could at least spell the word, even if they weren't knowledgeable about it. It was only natural then, that Muriel and I gravitated to each other. She too, became involved with helping me in my small "kitchen-office", sending literature to all points. She was a sparkplug for us as we spread our wings and soared with our organization. Muriel was an antique buff and I learned a great deal about her special interest.

These three special people - Fran, Carol and Muriel, were like priceless treasures to me. What I had anticipated to be an empty life, surprisingly, because of them became very full and I was not unhappy. Yes, Minneapolis was where I belonged.

When I would attend our National Board meetings, I met very attractive, interesting people and we became close friends. It never occurred to me to think of any one of the men in any other way. Once in a while one of them might ask me to have dinner with him, but again it was always a "business" arrangement. My family teased me on occasion, but I gave them to understand that I was not interested. I was not looking for a man. Besides, I still had a husband - in a way.

I had been in Washington, D.C. for a meeting and of course, the press were always on hand to do interviews. Their stories circulated around the territory. Shortly after my trip there, I went to the mailbox for my mail. I couldn't have been more surprised to find a letter from my childhood friend and boyfriend in high school, Gordon, and his wife DeLoris, whom I also knew from another small town near Wolsey. She had sometimes dated Ken in high school, so we all knew each other. They had read the story about me and what I was doing so they wrote to inquire about it. It was almost like a dream - that I would hear from them after forty years of not knowing the whereabouts of each other.

I told my daughters of the letter I had received and what a strange coincidence it was. We all laughed about it and they made jokes about an old "romance rekindled".

I wrote to Gordon and DeLoris and explained my involvement with ADRDA, and that began a continuing correspondence with them. They invited me to let them know when I came that way the next time and said perhaps we could meet for dinner. Several times we attempted to carry out our plans but something always seemed to get in the way. First and foremost, I then learned that DeLoris was ill.

As time passed,the messages from them were very discouraging because her condition was worsening. Cancer is a cruel fate and it was relentless in her case. As she became unable to communicate with me, Gordon and I stayed in touch because we truly understood each other's pain. We were both completely helpless and were destined to "stand by" and watch the suffering and deterioration of our loved one.

At a surprisingly early date the word came that DeLoris had lost the fight. We could only be grateful that her agony had come to an end. Naturally, Gordon was in shock and questioned what path his life would take. His home had been in Wilmington, Delaware, for many years. His work with DuPont had been there and so were his friends. Also, his son, Michael and family lived nearby. Kay, his daughter, a single parent with two fine boys, lived in Florida. He and DeLoris had planned for many years that when retirement came, they would spend their winters in Florida. Now with this turn of events, where should he go and what should he do?

Gordon's mother-in-law had been living in Wilmington in her own apartment, and now with the likelihood of Gordon not being there permanently, it became necessary to consider alternative arrangements for her. After several months, and because of her advanced age and decline in health, a nursing home seemed to be the answer. Her wish was to return to the Midwest, hopefully to South Dakota, her former home. Gordon made plans to make a visit to his niece's in Minneapolis and to Huron, South Dakota, to inquire about possible care facilities. He telephoned me and told me of his impending visit and asked if we might have lunch for old times' sake. Lunch! With a man? Good heavens, did I dare? I had not had a social conversation with a man for so many years I wasn't sure I could even handle it intelligently. Yet, I was curious and I knew it could be very pleasant to renew such a longtime friendship that had been "put on hold" for years. Again, I explained the situation to my daughters, and their answer, "Mother, you have every right to have lunch with an old friend - male or female - and allow yourself to enjoy it." With that in mind, I accepted.

15

The day came for Gordon to arrive and I was as nervous as a cat on a tin roof. When he came to the door, it was a real revelation. Where were those two young, skinny kids that we remembered? We were both considerably heavier, or putting it nicely, more "mature looking". We both wore glasses, and my grey hair was a dead giveaway. His "carrot top" had faded also. We couldn't help but have a good laugh. Our luncheon was an absolute delight - reminiscing about the "good old days", our families and the crazy things we'd done as kids. The time flew. Later, Gordon called to say his niece had tickets to a musical and asked if I cared to join them. Of course, he already knew that music had been a big part of my life so it was exciting to be included. It turned out to be "The Best Little Whorehouse in Texas". What a "happening" for a first evening out! Anyway, it was a most enjoyable one. We had many laughs about our choice of "cultural" entertainment. Another evening the four of us went to a soccer game - the first I'd ever seen in my life. It surely was different and pleasant to be in mixed company.

I had mentioned that I was invited to a 50th wedding anniversary of dear friends in Watertown, South Dakota, that weekend. I had a ride out with a friend but as there was no way to get back, I probably would have to send my regrets. Gordon then said he would also be in South Dakota at that time, and if I'd like, he'd come back to Minneapolis through Watertown and I could ride home with him. I especially wanted to attend this special gathering of my friend's, so it was a wonderful opportunity.

I went to Watertown and it was a nostalgic affair with many of my dear friends in attendance, some of which I had not seen in some time.

The next day, Gordon came for me at my friend's house and we had a chance, as we drove, to have a longer visit about our lives. I was sincerely concerned about his future, for I'd been told that men were especially vulnerable after losing a mate. I stressed to him the importance of being cautious of women who were eager to find a companion. I didn't want him to be "taken in" by some conniving female. I told him now that he was available, they would be on his doorstep. He was good-looking, interesting, personable, intelligent, fun-loving with a great sense of humor and he had done well in his lifetime. He had many desirable qualities so I kept urging him to "beware"! He listened and assured me he'd remember that.

It came time for Gordon to return to Wilmington and my social life in mixed company came to a close. It was surely fun while it lasted. We continued to correspond, usually sending each other ridiculous greeting cards relating to any experience we'd shared at some time.

I was due for a trip to Philadelphia to speak to a newly organized Alzheimer chapter and Gordon agreed to meet me. Wilmington is very close so he made reservations for me at a hotel there. He wanted me to meet his son and family, which I did. He and I had dinner at the Wilmington Country Club, where elegant dining is the norm. Another evening he took me to the Green Room in the DuPont building, and again I felt like a queen. They had live music, our style, and we danced together for the first time since high school. It was delightful. Then, once again, it all came to an end and it was time for me to go back to reality and to my apartment in Minneapolis All of this time I was feeling guilty because I realized I had actually enjoyed myself. I told myself I must not encourage this any longer. Gordon had already given me a surprise gift for old times' sake - a plain silver ring on a chain to wear around my neck. I cherished it and often reflected back on the little silver ring I had lost many years before.

Days and weeks passed and my work piled higher and higher as the word about Alzheimer's spread and the demand was greater for more information and help for families. I traveled nearly every week. When I arrived at my destination, I sometimes had several interviews with the press, T.V. appearances, meetings at breakfast, lunch and dinner as well as public presentations. I didn't notice how exhausting it was until my return home. I seemed to thrive on the excitement.

The holidays were approaching and the plan was that I would spend Christmas in Orlando, Florida, with Sharee's family. Strangely enough, Gordon had made plans to visit his daughter, Kay, and her boys in Coral Springs, Florida, at the same time. On my arrival at Sharee's, there were one dozen beautiful red roses awaiting me! What a romantic surprise. My family really began to wonder.

Mitzi and John had already met Gordon when he was in

Minneapolis, but Sharee had not as yet. The girls thought it was great fun to finally meet this Gordon that they had heard my mother and me speak of all their lives. They assured me that it was o.k. for me to see him as I'd been doing. Sharee even invited him to come to Orlando during his stay in Florida and he accepted without hesitation. My mother-in-law and Sharee's mother-in-law were visiting there as well, and when Gordon arrived, they were both peering out the front window and met him at the door before I was even aware he was there! What a stitch! It was an ice-breaker and a good laugh. We had a wonderful time. Three days later, my birthday was extra special, with Gordon still there. He made a hit all around. I later learned that my daughters began telephoning each other and were asking, "What do you think Mom is up to?"

16

My mind began to feel boggled between trips to visit Ken, who hadn't spoken nor recognized us for a number of years, appointments for Alzheimer's seminars to make presentations and an occasional meeting with Gordon whenever it could be arranged. I could not seem to explain why I found myself laughing when I should be crying and crying when I should be laughing. My emotions were scrambled and it was a bit frightening. When Gordon and I were driving along together, we sang to the tops of our voices and yet I hadn't been able to sing a note for years, even though I'd sung in choirs since I was eleven years old. I couldn't believe this was happening, and always a sense of guilt came over me. I only knew that I had feelings I didn't know I had.

My 86 year-old mother-in-law came to visit and I explained to her that I was afraid of myself, for Gordon and I seemed so right when we were together but I was not free to even think that way. I shall never forget the strength that came to me when she said, "Bobbie, you have been a widow long enough. Now you have a chance for happiness and I think you should take it." This was a profound statement for a mother whose only child was a victim of Alzheimer's. The weight of the world seemed to be lifted. Gordon and I were well aware that we would like to live out our lives together. I hadn't thought it possible and a few months previously, I'd have said "no way". I had never dreamed I'd ever have a man in my life again and I had made it clear to everyone that I was content with my life alone. How wrong could one be?

Gordon's children found it more difficult to accept me, for Gordon hadn't been alone very long. I could understand that. My children had already given me their blessing. What his children did not realize was how comfortable we were together due to the closeness of our families through the years and our feelings for each other long ago.

Within a short time all of our offspring acknowledged the inevitable. However, the fact remained that I was not free to marry. The word "divorce" sent chills through me and I was not sure I could go through with it. My daughters both said,

"Mother, you are not hurting anyone." We all knew we'd lost their father years before. Yet, I vacillated as I thought about it and even sent Gordon away at one time when he came to see me. He was crushed and I was heartbroken as well, for in my heart, I did not want him to leave. I confided in several of my good friends in ADRDA and told them of my dilemma. I quickly learned that this kind of situation was not new to others in our organization. I could not believe how naive I had been. Some were living with companions of the opposite sex even though they still cared and were responsible for the welfare of their spouses. We were many lonely people and I hadn't realized it. As for me, divorce was the only answer. It had to be legal and above-board. It was the most difficult and traumatic decision I'd made during my lifetime.

I contacted a lawyer friend and initiated proceedings. It was a curious feeling to go about this with no other party involved. It was relatively simple and carefully planned so as to make it the least painful, but at times I kept hearing in my mind my marriage vows and wondered if it was the right thing to do. Then again I thought "Yes, I do have a right to happiness."

The appointed day came for me to appear in court and I felt I must be dreaming. My dear friend, Muriel, went with me. Within five minutes, 41 years of marriage came to an end. Incredible. I felt totally numb and we barely said a word to each other on the way home. It was done and now I had to turn the page and begin a new chapter.

17

Excitement prevailed as our wedding plans unfolded. My intent now was to make it a happy time for both of us as we'd suffered enough. This wonderful man who had come back into my life deserved the best, and I wanted to do everything in my power to make that happen. The date was set - April 18, 1981. My friends were buzzing because of all the stir I was creating. It was SO romantic! My dear and very special friend, Fran, planned a dinner party so that the "girls" could see if they approved of Gordon. Three of my closest friends were there to greet him. He didn't mind being the only man in the group for he could well hold his own when put to the test. He got a big kick out of it. Fran, the hostess, met him with the words, "If you marry Bobbie, you get us all!" It was hilarious. Later on, Fran gave a bridal shower for me. Such fun! I even modeled the beautiful nightie and negligee that they gave me. I kept thinking all of this fuss must be for someone else.

We would have a quiet ceremony, plain and simple with just our immediate families attending. It would take place in Sharee's yard on her beautiful patio in Orlando. She arranged for the minister and flowers as well as the place for our luncheon afterwards at a downtown hotel. She also prepared a ton of food for munching on later in the day. I had written a song, dedicated to Gordon, and recorded it. It would be played as we took our places. I called it "New Beginnings":

New beginnings from an old romance,
New beginnings gave a second chance.
What we thought was just a memory
Brought us back to a reality.
Time stood still, and then we parted -
Time stood still and then we started over.
When we found our love was always there,
It was meant for us to live and share.
New beginnings from now on will be
New beginnings 'till eternity.

Each of our children had a part in the ceremony as well as our grandchildren. Gordon had asked me the kind of ring I would like and my answer was "I already have it - the little silver ring I've been wearing around my neck." I felt like Cinderella. This was a first meeting for all of our children and it was a beautiful and unforgettable moment as we formed a circle and all joined hands in prayer - our wonderful expanded family.

Mitzi was expecting a first baby so that was an added thrill. She and John had been married quite a long time, and after two tragic and unfortunate pregnancies, this was a hopeful time. Kay had two boys, Michael had two boys, and Sharee had a boy and a girl.

Gordon carried out his dream of having a place in Florida and had purchased a villa at Bonaventure near Ft. Lauderdale. The plan was that we would spend a few winter months there and the rest of the time in Minneapolis in my small apartment. He sold his home in Wilmington and agreed to come back to the Midwest where it all began.

The wedding took place - a perfect day and a gorgeous setting. The grandchildren thought it was really funny to see Gramps kissing Grandma. They had a great time throwing rice and decorating our car, even to the tin cans tied on the back. We felt like two school kids.

We were in our home at Bonaventure when Sharee and Al paid us a visit. It was discovered that Al was ill and it was of concern to all of us. He returned home and was admitted to the hospital where he was diagnosed as having severe brittle diabetes. We were all shocked, yet thankful that there would be help.

We returned to Minneapolis for the spring and summer and to be there for the arrival of little Benjamin David, August 20th. With Sharee's children quite grown up, it was very special to welcome a new boy into the family. It was exhilarating for this grandmother to once again experience the feel of that little bundle in my arms.

When we went back to Florida in the fall, I noticed that I did not seem to have the energy that I'd had and began limiting my duties with ADRDA. I experienced a peculiar spell while we were on a pleasure trip down to the Keys. We returned to Bonaventure immediately. We saw a doctor and I was hospitalized. He suggested that we return to Minneapolis and proceed with further medical testing. While undergoing the tests, I had a heart attack. (I do not intend to dwell on my health, but over the next three years I had six surgeries - one being open-heart - and two slight strokes.) Suddenly life seemed more precious than ever. I knew for sure that I was not superhuman and that perhaps my obsession with Alzheimer's had taken a toll. The stress of 16 years or more of our family's "endurance test" was apparent.

During a terminal illness, we try to prepare ourselves for the inevitable. I wonder if that is ever possible.

We knew that Ken was deteriorating rapidly and that he became more frail with each day, but when the final word came, it was difficult to comprehend the reality of it all. He slipped away peacefully and we rejoiced in that. His body had fought the good fight long after we realized he had much earlier left us. One cannot begin to empathize with the emotions that consume the family in such an experience unless it is someone who's "been there".

Even though I had made a new life for myself and did not focus on "looking back", there were sacred and beautiful memories never to be erased. It did not seem real to any of us, I'm sure.

A private graveside service was held with our two daughters each giving a eulogy to their father. It was exactly like he'd want.

In the meantime, Sharee and Al had been transferred to Omaha, Nebraska. They were sad to leave Florida and it would be another adjustment. John had become ill and it troubled us a great deal for him and Mitzi. There seemed to be unrest in that household and we hoped and prayed that the difficulty could be resolved. It was during this time that Mitzi anticipated the birth of a second child. It was a difficult period for all of us but we tried to feel positive that when the baby arrived, all would be well. On December 5th little Ian Alistair came into the world. He was a beautiful baby. With the boys just 15 months apart, Mitzi would have her hands full.

I think it only natural that we want happiness and the very best for our children. Many times when they are suffering, it hurts us as much as it does them. And so it was, a short time later, we learned that Mitzi and John were separating. It was like a nightmare.

During this turn of events, a friend and Alzheimer family member from Tennessee, whom I never met but had correspondence, sent me a sampler she had hand-embroidered. I cherish it for it is indeed a treasure. It hangs on the wall by my door where I am constantly reminded of its meaningful message. It is the familiar Serenity Prayer: "God grant me the serenity to accept the things I cannot change, the courage to change the things I can, and the wisdom to know the difference" Words to live by...

I had received emotional nourishment from my loving and caring family and we would continue to support each other in any crisis. Sharee was dealing with Al's illness and now Mitzi was alone with two very small boys. I was proud of the way they dealt with the reverses in their lives. We need to be open to lessons learned through pain. Again - it's not what happens TO you that makes the difference - it's what happens IN you.

18

Gordon and I vowed when we were married that we would live "one day at a time." We also said that if we had five happy years together, it was five more than we had had before.

My small apartment was o.k. until my "new roommate" moved in and then it was really cramped. We began searching for something more adequate and by chance, came upon a new condominium complex with which we fell in love. It was in a wooded area in Bloomington, a south suburb of Minneapolis, where little deer came almost to our door. We could feed them from our hands. It was beautiful any time of year and it had it all - a spacious party room, exercise room, large indoor swimming pool and underground garage with car-wash and fully equipped workshop and tennis courts. Another great feature were the two guest rooms that one might reserve for visitors. Our children and families came frequently or we went to visit them.

In between ill health and difficult problems, we enjoyed some special happy times. We took a bus tour with a group to the Canadian Rockies. It was superb. Gordon and I even went white-water rafting on the Snake River. What an experience! Besides the boat standing on end part of the time, I sat right over the space where water was to drain out. Instead, as we hit a wave, that icy cold mountain water came up under me! Talk about a shock! I wrote a song while traveling in which I named everyone on our bus and told of the places we visited. It proved to be a surprise the last night of the trip and it was fun for it was a complete log of our excursion. We met some wonderful friends with whom we continued to stay in touch.

Another year we took a bus tour to the New England states in the fall. The colors were glorious and it was every bit as beautiful as we'd always heard. One of the neatest evenings was in Bar Harbor, Maine, where we had a clam and lobster bake. We all wore huge bibs and enjoyed every morsel as butter dribbled down our chins.

Mitzi and John were divorced by this time and she continued her counseling at two community colleges. She also began working on her Master's degree. It was a load with two little boys of pre-school age.

Kay was a successful business woman who had raised two young men, David (Bo) and Steven, now approaching college age. We were very proud of her accomplishments. She was a wonderful mother.

Michael was an airline pilot who was highly respected in his profession. The real blow came for him at Christmas time in 1985, when his wife announced that she was filing for divorce. Just like that - as he was about to take little Bret and Aaron out to select their Christmas tree. It seemed unbelievable that three of our four children would now be divorced. Not a very impressive track record and a sad one indeed. Again we all rallied round and offered our love and support. If there was one thing we could be sure of in our family, it was love and caring - a real blessing that many families never know.

Sharee and Al led a busy life and a gratifying one with an avocation as family counselors in their church. Strange that both of my daughters and I were counseling in our own ways. Gordon called us "do-gooders" and I can only say that I didn't consider that all bad.

During the summer of '85 Gordon celebrated his big 7-0 birthday. Our children planned a real "bash". It was decided that the most appropriate place to gather was at CUSTER STATE PARK in our beautiful Black Hills of South Dakota - a place forever dear to our hearts. Such a birthday has been enjoyed by few. We were all there except our only granddaughter who had just begun a new job. We headquartered at Sylvan Lake Resort where we had individual cabins but came together for meals at the lodge. We hiked, went sight-seeing, rode horseback, saw all kinds of wild life, and literally inhaled the beauty of the Hills. The four little boys referred to Mt. Rushmore as "George, Tom, Teddy and Abe". The four "big little boys" posed for pictures imitating the four faces, and then turned around, leaned over a brick wall and posed as they thought the Presidents would look from the back side! They wore special t-shirts with a picture of four bare derrieres hanging over a cliff. Two small children were looking up at them. One said, "I don't know where we are but we MUST be somewhere behind Mt. Rushmore." Needless to say, they created quite a sensation. Such nonsense but such fun!

Life seemed to be going by so fast that sometimes we felt we'd like to "stop the world" for a while.

We had been dissatisfied with our location at Bonaventure in Florida and decided to sell and purchase another place - a manufactured home on the gulf side at North Fort Myers. It was a beautiful and most adequate house overlooking a small lake and a golf course. Retirement was so involved that Gordon often jokingly said he should perhaps go back to work for then he would at least have his Saturdays and Sundays off. He loved the outdoor life - fishing and golfing, and time with our friends. We shared many joys.

I kept busy with P.E.O., friends and a continuing involvement with ADRDA, even though health problems continued to plague me. My counseling never ceased, and my thrust was to assure care-givers that they did have a right to happiness and they must take care of themselves. My "magnificent obsession" had come about because of my own needs. It had been a "lifeline" for me and the most gratifying thing I had ever done. The tragedy of Alzheimer's and Related Diseases was finally hopeful for thousands of families. A negative problem was now looking forward to a positive solution.

19

There were special times too. Gordon and I had two unusual trips to New York City that were a thrill for us. Because Rita Hayworth was a victim of Alzheimer's Disease, her daughter, Princess Yasmin Aga Kahn, who is a member of our National Board, planned a gala in her mother's honor in order to raise funds for ADRDA. It became an annual affair to which many celebrities and people of substance came. We too were invited and took our only granddaughter, Jody, one time and our grandson, Mark, the next. It was exciting for us and even moreso for Jody and Mark to mingle with such an affluent and impressive group at these extravaganzas. Jody met a princess and danced the night away with a millionaire's son. Mark was both surprised and pleased when Kathryn Crosby congratulated me for having such a handsome grandson. It was a once in a life-time experience for us to be in a position to take them to such a beautiful ball.

I also attended the initial meeting in Washington, D.C., to organize an International Association for Alzheimer's. The name chosen was Alzheimer's Disease International (ADI). A number of countries were represented and although they came with enthusiasm, they looked to us as a model for we had already experienced the "starting up" process. The first official meeting took place in Belgium where I had been invited to participate, but my health did not permit such extensive travel. The following year they met in Paris. Once agan the distance was too great for me to attend. In 1987, the meeting was set for Chicago. I knew it probably would never be as close again so I made plans to go. It was awesome to be in the presence of people from many other parts of the world, some with whom I had corresponded, all there with one purpose - that of combating Alzheimer's Disease. Now it was proven that it was a universal problem.

Our Annual Meeting and National Board Meeting in Chicago was a festive occasion - our 8th birthday - celebrated with balloons, live music for dancing, and a generally good time. This is not usually the case with these meetings as there is much work to be done. It was a mix of business and pleasure. The occasion was humbling to be honored with volunteer founders who had a vision and made things happen. It was also an emotional moment reflecting on the many accomplishments that began with a handful of dedicated people and now were in vast numbers. I truly believe that with all the interest and general concern, there is bound to be an answer to this insidious disease and the burden it poses on the family. I hope to see that day.

Another phase of my life began taking place. Grandma Glaze was still living in Clark, South Dakota, on her 90th birthday. Sharee and Mitzi planned a huge birthday party for her so that her special friends of many years could help her celebrate. It was a beautiful event and she was amazed at the number of friends who came from some distance as well as the home folks. She looked radiant with her pretty pink corsage and her jaunty pink suit. It was obvious though that her vision had diminished to a point that was worrisome to her neighbors. Of special concern was her management of the stove for she was unable to see if it was on or off.

We returned to Minneapolis pondering how we might resolve this problem. Within a few weeks we learned that she had fallen several times. We visited her and asked if she would consider moving to Minneapolis if we could find an appropriate home for her. This was my responsibility as Ken had been an only child and she relied on me. She had always had a mind of her own, but now realized this was a necessary step and very willingly agreed to the change. Fortunately I found a place for her at Augustana Home. I'm sure it was a difficult adjustment, but she never complained. I was most grateful for she was closer and it would be more convenient for us to visit her and manage her affairs. She won the admiration and respect of all the staff at the Home.

All went well even though her rapid decline was evident. One morning as she was dressing for breakfast she fell and broke her hip. She recovered from the surgery but by the time she was able to return to the Home, that perky, spunky little lady who had always been extremely independent was a different person. Having never been ill in her life, she simply did not know how to cope. I often thought about how impatient we were with her through the years because of her stubbornness. Later, I realized that she had not wanted to be a burden to anyone and that is an admirable trait. Our family was saddened to see her in such a weakened condition, resulting in a deterioration that utimately led to her death. She had lived a full life and at age 92 was ready. We were grateful there was no long-term lingering and suffering. Another chapter came to a close.

20

Life goes on, and looking back, I wondered where the time had gone. I did not ever think of myself as being seventy years old. My children always said they knew no one who fought old age as much as their mother. I was not overjoyed when it was time for me to apply for social security. My friend, Puggy, came for me and insisted I get that accomplished. From a practical aspect, we both knew that it was necessary, but I cringed at the thought of being labeled a senior citizen. That was o.k. for old folks but I could not get excited about all the wonderful "benefits" for which I would now be eligible.

I remember when I graduated from high school a little old grey haired neighbor-friend gave me two companion pictures which she had hand-painted. I was thrilled with such a fine gift because I felt it was remarkable for her at age seventy to be able to perform such a feat.

December 28th, 1987, was fast approaching and that big day was to be a family celebration. It was meant to be a surprise, but with our expanded family scattered in all directions, and plans to be made, they decided to let me in on it. The children all said, "We can't keep anything from Mom."

Our only granddaughter, Jody, who goes to school in Minneapolis and is employed at the Marriott Hotel as a reservationist, was in charge of arrangements. And what arrangements! She reserved a block of rooms with a beautiful suite for all of us. So to the Marriott we all moved for the entire weekend. It was fastastic!

Michael flew in from his Singapore run, meeting his little boys, Aaron and Bret, from Pennsylvania in Chicago, and brought them to Minneapolis. Kay, friend Tony, and her boys, Steve and David, flew in from Florida. Sharee, Alan and son Mark drove from Omaha, Nebraska, and of course Mitzi and her two cherubs, Ben and Ian, were already in the metro area as well as our organizer, Jody. My sister-in-law, Mildred, her daughter Barbara and husband Ed, all came from Iowa. I'm sure the Marriott probably never before had experienced such a "Birthday Bash." A glorious affair!

The last evening was the "official dinner." Besides the

immediate family, Gordon's niece, Bev and husband, Al, came as well as my cousin, Stan and wife, Marian. Also in attendance was my good friend, Muriel. The dinner was pool-side (they had closed off the pool for us) which is a very attractive area. White linen, beautifully appointed with bouquets of Christmas greens with white mums, holly and candlelight set the scene. It was a picture. Gordon had his video camera available and our "very professional" grandson, Mark, was the photographer for this "social event of the season."

Following the dinner we all retired to our "hospitality room" where we viewed the pictures taken at the dinner. Incredible! There was also an "opening" for everyone had brought gifts. Such fun for someone whose birthday gift had always been under the Christmas tree with all the other gifts. I shall forever cherish the memories.

After never before having a birthday party in all the years of my life, and then to have one such as this, I decided that perhaps it really wasn't as painful as I'd expected when the big "seven-oh" rolled around!

21

As I reflect back on the years, it is probably understandable that a great part of my life focused on Alzheimer's disease and related disorders and the impact on the thousands of families that were victimized.

In the beginning, I searched desperately for a clue as to some one person who would perhaps also have an afflicted family member, or hopefully, a professional - any care-professional who would be knowledgeable and more importantly, sympathetic and caring. I chose to bare my soul and tell our family's story. My wish was to dispel the same kind of stigma that persisted with mental illness. There was a strong compulsion to pursue a course of action in order to locate families with similar needs.

An "organization kit" was designed with "dos and don'ts" of starting up support groups and tips on the necessary procedures. A "network" evolved which connected families and reassured them that there were ways to survive. There would be resources to turn to for help once we could educate the world about our dilemma. I soon learned that one's station in life - rich or poor, royalty or common ordinary people - was not a consideration. Those from all walks of life came to us. No one could claim immunity. Naturally, our needs varied. The wealthy grieved as their family member deteriorated and they watched helplessly, but they could afford around-the-clock care. Then there were families who had lost everything, being reduced to begging for help while grieving for their loved one.

We began with a handful of people where it was possible to offer guidance and direction on a one-to-one basis. We were a self-help, non-profit, unique organization - totally volunteer and for the most part, care givers. There was a willingness to give selflessly of themselves in any way possible without neglecting their patient at home. Love simply exuded among us, making it very special. I regret that as our growth far surpassed our expectations, it became more difficult to deal quite so personally, even though we continued to strive for that quality. Our families needed help - and now. They were the heart of our Association. Fortunately, with more committed volunteers, professionals and trained staff, every effort was made to reach out whenever and wherever necessary. We realized we must never lose sight of our reason for being.

A number of people - some very prominent - traveled to Minneapolis to talk to someone who would listen and understand. One man was chief counsel for the U. S. House of Representatives Operation Committee in Washington D. C. Another was an anthropologist who had lived all over the world. Interesting people came from all points. A young woman whose husband was diagnosed at age 40, pleaded for help. Her baby was one year old. They grasped at every straw for information because they had been given none. We did not advise but guided and explored options together.

So many stories come to mind. It is very nostalgic thinking back on what I heard as people contacted me by corredpondence or telephone. A friend in California wrote, "My teenage children are upset because their father doesn't remember conversations." Some said, "I devoured your literature." One of the most poignant letters was from a woman in New Mexico who wrote, "This is our wedding anniversary. My husband is in a mental hospital and doesn't know who I am." An older man in West Virginia called to tell me that he felt as though he were in jail - couldn't leave for a minute. There were others who were in a panic because they had been forced to sell their homes, had nothing left and couldn't even get food stamps. I heard over and over, "I read your story many times and cried - I thought I could have written it myself." Some people called many places trying to locate me and when they did find me they asked, "May I join your organization? You are my one hope of being helpful to others." I was known for my "folksy ways" and the many postcards I mailed to let someone know I was thinking of them or to answer a question. I did not have enough hours in my day - or night - to write letters to everyone.

A daughter telephoned our home while I was away and talked to Gordon. She explained that her father was a care-giver who refused to ask for help and his own health was failing. She asked if I would please telephone him and reason with him, not letting him know that she had initiated the call. She lived in Denver and he lived in Iowa so it was impossible for her to manage the problem at such a distance. I immediately made the call, beginning by inquiring about the status of his wife's illness. I often did this when I learned of a new person who needed support. We visited and then began correspondence as well as follow-up calls. I pointed out to him how worrisome it was for families when geographically far apart. They too must be considered. He listened and before long agreed to finding a care facility. I felt the daughter actually saved his life for he learned to "let go" and freed himself to spend time with family and friends and yet visit his wife as he chose. In my opinion it was a healthy decision.

Someone once said, "The most important place is where you now find yourself, the most important deed is the one which awaits you now, and the most important person is the one who is closest to you in this moment and needs you."

My emphasis was always on the care-giver and positive ways to "get on" with life. Our people needed to know how to "accept" and prepare for the future realistically. Self-pity had no place among us. I learned through my work with REACH and ADRDA that I had been blessed with God-given strengths previously unknown to me. They had not been tapped and put to use. It is my belief that through tragedy we are given opportunities and we must choose how we'll deal with them. There comes a time when we must move on and encourage others to do the same. I simply opened one door and doors opened to me from that day on, all because I listened from the heart.

Many places in my home are favorite quotes as reminders such as one by Barrie, "Those who bring sunshine to the lives of others cannot keep it from themselves." There are others by anonymous writers: "I am not afraid of tomorrow for I have seen yesterday and I love today." Another favorite is "You have to believe in the birds that grow. Believe in the grass in the damp of snow. Ah, that is the reason a bird can sing. On the darkest day he believes in spring."

I've said repeatedly that many of the things that happened in my early life helped prepare me for later years. The children of my day had grown up knowing hardship and what it was to "go without". Yet, we were content and appreciated values materially and philosophically. We respected authority and we learned to cope even though things weren't always the way we'd like them to be. More importantly, we learned that one doesn't give up when the going is rough. At times I had felt like a fish on a hook - trapped - but if I struggled hard enough, it might be possible to break loose. When my children learned I was writing the story of my life, they said, "Mom, what will you call it?" Jokingly, I answered, "I think I'll name it 'The First Seventy Years Are the Hardest'." We all had a good laugh over that.

Through the "ups and downs", my life was enriched beyond measure all along the way. I was fortunate in having a solid family background, an unusual growth experience during my childhood, a valued education, a happy marriage for many years with Ken, beautiful children and grandchildren, and later an important challenge that gave me a purpose, and health for many years to carry out the work of REACH and ADRDA. I was given a chance for new beginnings when Gordon came back into my life - indeed a blessing. I had friends everywhere. I thought I must be the richest person in the world. My hope is that others - each in his own way - may find encouragement and strive for the happiness they deserve and to which they have a right.

Joseph Epstein in his wisdom said, "We do not choose to be born. We do not choose our parents. We do not choose our own historical epoch or the country of our birth or the immediate circumstances of upbringing. We do not - most of us - choose to die. Nor do we choose the time or condition of our death, but within all this realm of choicelessness, we do choose how we shall live: courageously or in cowardice, honorably or dishonorably, with purpose or in drift. We decide what is important and what is trivial in life. We decide that what makes us significant is either what we do or what we refuse to do. But no matter how indifferent the universe may be to our choices or decisions, these choices and decisions are ours to make. We decide, we choose, and as we decide and choose so are our lives formed."

This is an accounting of the life of a prairie girl. I did not choose some of the things that happened along the way but I am grateful for every day and every growth experience. My choice is to live out my life to the fullest. There is no doubt - I choose to continue.